FROM DESPAIR TO BELOVED

FROM DESPAIR TO BELOVED:
The Provocative Cinema of On Mark Productions

by SCOTT KENYON BARKER
with MARK BARANOWSKI

BearManor Media
2015

From Despair to Beloved:
The Provocative Cinema of On Mark Productions

©2015 Scott Kenyon Barker, Mark Baranowski

All rights reserved.

Front cover photo: Ryli Morgan, photo courtesy of
Rick Rorie/Baranowski Archive.

Title page photo: Mark Baranowski and Rachelle Williams in *Heaven Help Me, I'm in Love* (2005), photo courtesy of Baranowski Archive.

Back cover photos (courtesy Baranowski Archive):
Despair VHS box cover art; *Hardly Beloved* poster & DVD box cover art.

For information, address:

BearManor Media
P. O. Box 71426
Albany, GA 31708

bearmanormedia.com

Typesetting and layout by John Teehan

Published in the USA by BearManor Media

ISBN—1-59393-860-8
978-1-59393-860-4

LCCN: 2015912672

Image courtesy of: Baranowski Archive.

Table of Contents

Foreword	ix
Introduction: Takin' (Film) to the Streets	1
Chapter One: *Despair*	5
Chapter Two: *Ryli Morgan: Audition*	17
Chapter Three: *Runaway Terror*	23
Chapter Four: *The Zombie Room*	39
Chapter Five: *Expendable*	49
Chapter Six: *Sin by Murder*	61
Chapter Seven: *The Powerful Play*	77
Chapter Eight: *Heaven Help Me, I'm in Love*	87
Chapter Nine: *Ill Times*	109
Chapter Ten: *Mister Dissolute*	121
Chapter Eleven: *Hardly Beloved*	135
Appendix One: *Hardly Beloved* shooting script	149
Appendix Two: Scott Interviews Mark and Ryli	245
Appendix Three: Words From the Players	253
About the Authors	267

Foreword

I BECAME AWARE of the cinema of Mark Baranowski due to my fondness for films lensed in Florida. I'm not sure why, but Florida horror movies, exploitation films, even the nudie cuties and nudist colony films from way back hold a fascination for me. Strange, since I've been to Florida and find it to be too hot, too bright, and full of creatures that will try to eat you. Sure, we have a few bears in Michigan, and the occasional mountain lion, but they have prehistoric reptiles down there! Sheesh!

Anyway, my editor, Mark Engle of *Cultcuts* magazine, sent me a film that had a pretty girl on it, a knife, and someone in a blank mask. I'm a huge fan of the slasher genre, and this was released in 2002—before the glut on the market of idiots everywhere trying to make a movie, regardless of talent.

It was called *Runaway Terror*. I liked it. I liked Ryli Morgan, and thought she was very pretty. Later, I would learn that she was actually Mark's wife, Teresa. As I said, pretty. Pretty is always a good thing in a slasher flick. This one made you think, and I appreciate using my brain in the slasher genre. Plus, I thought it was shot in Florida.

In later conversation with Mark, I discovered that its true location was North Carolina. Okay, that's fine. Good to know.

At around the same time, I was writing reviews for almost everything released by Alternative Cinema, home of the delectable actress, Misty Mundae. One of the discs included an extra feature, called *Despair*. I recognized Baranowski's name on the flick and decided to watch it. Um, yeah, this short film was aptly titled. I felt so bad for Mark and Ryli in this film. Of course, I knew they were only acting, but it was just so damned downbeat. To be honest, I haven't watched it since.

After that, I got to know more about Mark. I interviewed him for my zine, *Divine Exploitation*. I interviewed Ryli in another issue. They were cool folks, and I learned that Mark was also a musician.

I wasn't surprised. Musicians take time to craft their product, going over it again and again, polishing and polishing until they're, at the very least, happy to let others listen to it. You can see that craft in Mark's films, as well.

From there, four films came in fast and furious succession:

Expendable tells of a drug dealer that's ready to call it quits. He just has to make a visit to his estranged wife, with murder on his mind. However, as is the case in many of Baranowski's movies, there's something in store that you never see coming.

Sin by Murder brings that classic "Skinemax" steam to the table on a budget that wouldn't cover the cost of merkins (Look it up!) on a Cinemax production. It's steamy, bloody, and Mark and Ryli make such a great pair of cops investigating a murder. My favorite scene would have to be when they give the suspect a lie detector test. It looks pretty good, and the scene is done well. Then you notice, once it's all over, that there is no actual machine! This is innovation at its core. The entire film is so well done that it remains a favorite of mine, to this day.

The Powerful Play is a series of music videos that allow Mark to express his music in a visual medium. It's a great insight into how an artist's brain works.

Finally, we have *Heaven Help Me, I'm in Love*. While the horror community had no problems embracing Mark's films, he's not really a "horror movie" kind of guy. He makes what interests him. This time, we get a sweet romantic comedy. In the land of micro-budget filmmaking, this just isn't done. It's comparable to the work of Mendon, Massachusetts filmmaker Michael Legge, who makes comedy after comedy—all of them brilliant, and all of them severely under-watched by the world at large. Baranowski proves that he's not restricted by genre in this film, which actually jabs at the whole micro-budget process, as well.

Still, this wasn't Mark's last film. Next came *Ill Times*, four long years later. It may be the grittiest and most "urban" of what he's done to date. His musical persona, Marquis, is brought to the forefront here, with a layering of music that is integral to the plot.

Mark gives us more urban drama with a hard-boiled edge in the form of *Mister Dissolute*, made right after *Ill Times*. Put these two together and you've got the perfect double feature.

Finally, *Hardly Beloved* is Mark's autobiography, of sorts. While watching it, you can tell that he poured a lot of himself onto the page when he wrote the script.

I've met Mark and Teresa in person only once. It was at a small convention in Pittsburgh, where I also remember meeting Joe Bob Briggs for the first (and only) time. Teresa was severely pregnant. Having helped father five kids, I'm pretty good at giving pregnant wife advice, so I told them to keep her feet up and she'd be fine. Mark and I talked for quite a while about movies we loved, movies of his that I loved, and why I loved them. I made some special issues of *Divine Exploitation* for Teresa to give out to her "Ryli Morgan" fans. She really liked those.

Overall, it was a great time. Being able to talk to someone else intelligently about film always makes it better, and I'm glad that Mark and Teresa were there. They made the convention, for me.

The chasm of miles between Michigan and North Carolina are long, and although people in the micro-budget arena of filmmaking and film writing are infamous for their complete lack of external funds, I would love to visit with the Baranowskis again. I think I still owe Mark a copy of my film, *Gingersquatch*, for which I used his music during a metaphorical sex scene. It would be nice to deliver it in person.

Besides, then I could pitch him my idea about a sequel to the 1957 film, *The Astounding She-Monster*. Ryli Morgan would have to play the titular creature, and it would be awesome.

– Douglas Waltz,
Kalamazoo, Michigan

Mark, Douglas and Ryli (September 2006). Photo: Baranowski Archive.

Introduction

Takin' (Film) to the Streets

"YOU DON'T MAKE UP for your sins in church. You do it in the streets."

When Martin Scorsese wrote that line for *Mean Streets* more than forty years ago, he could have been talking about film.

You don't pay your dues in film school. You do it out on the pavement, in full view of the world.

Few can attest to this more so than Mark Baranowski and Ryli Morgan, two indie cinema survivors with the scars to prove that they've earned their bones through bare-knuckle filmmaking, down the boulevards and up the avenues.

I have known the real-life couple for about a dozen years, and watched them struggle with getting their creative visions out to the masses. I not only like them very much as people, I greatly respect them as colleagues. I understand the difficulty in what they have done. Picture a gymnastics routine at the Olympics where each apparatus is set on fire. It's like that.

As a fellow filmmaker, I have dealt with it all: the long hours; the cold pizza; the nightmare of trying to schedule a shoot while dealing with everyone's work schedule/family life/travel plans.

I have had relationships end, family members die, and had to sell houses and move, all in the midst of production.

There's never enough money... or time... or pairs of willing hands to chip in.

Actors drop out. Essential dialogue is obliterated by a dog barking, a car revving, or the pounding techno-trash tunes from a nightclub just feet away from your location.

Equipment freezes up in the cold, just when you need it. Your brain takes a cue from the camera/mike/recorder and goes into hibernation, from which five double espressos couldn't wake you.

Tempers flare. The person who said you could use his office/home/parking lot as a location suddenly begins to have second thoughts. You start to wonder if you can salvage both the movie and the friendship.

Every film shoot results in you asking, "Why am I putting myself through this?"

I recall being at the sharp end of an eighteen-hour shoot in a converted meat packing plant, pondering how many of the numerous pages of script we tried to cover that night but had to pass over, and whether we could get all of the actors back to shoot coverage on another night. (The answer to the last question was, sadly, no.)

I was ready to sit down and laugh—the sort of hysterical sound that overtakes you right before a nurse pushes the plunger on a hypodermic and you quickly get very quiet and compliant.

My shoelaces were untied and I was too tired to fix them. There was the stink in my nostrils of fake "charred bodies" EFX spray. My feeble calculations told me if I crashed in half an hour, I would only get, at best, two hours sleep before we all had to get up and shoot additional scenes at another location.

Yet, somewhere in the rusty tin can of my head, a tiny voice was saying, *You're making a movie!*

It's worth noting that most people on this planet will never know that feeling. They will watch movies, discuss them, dissect them, savage them, but they won't ever call "Action!" and listen to someone speak the words they've written.

If you have had that experience, then you know the privilege comes at a high price to your bank account, your sanity, and often to your relationships.

Although he certainly could have, it was not Scorsese who wrote, "That he which hath no stomach to this fight, let him depart." Shakespeare understood a thing or two about the ways in which the creative process mimics battle. If the Bard from Avon had been transported to a modern indie film set, he would have discovered the bitter truth of the movies—there are no Cheese Doodles left in the craft services box by the time the writer gets there, and rewriting is a never-ending process.

My job here, however, is not to point out the futilities in having an indie film career, but to celebrate the fact that it, indeed, *can be done.*

Mark and Ryli are proof of that.

Beginning with *Despair*, Mark wrote, produced and directed a group of movies that show both an impressive stylistic range, as well as a dedication that every serious micro-budget auteur would do well to emulate.

They are all worth a closer look, so, without further ado, here are some of the filmmaking lessons that we can take from Mark's movies.

And as they say at birthday parties, "May there be many more."

– Scott Kenyon Barker
Tucson, Arizona
January 2015

VHS box cover art. Photo: Baranowski Archive.

1

Despair

Release date: October 7, 2001
Director: Mark Baranowski
Writer: Mark Baranowski
Producer: Mark Baranowski
Music: MARQUIS (Mark Baranowski)
Genre: Drama, Horror
Runtime: 35 minutes
Cast: Mark Baranowski, Ryli Morgan, Bonzai
Plot: A married couple's final day, before each commits suicide. The man no longer wishes to live a life in which his artistic talents continue to go unrecognized and unappreciated. The woman has no desire to live without him, and her depression drives her to both insanity and self-destruction.

SKB: It's probably no accident that the title of this film sounds like a Fritz Lang silent. *Despair* takes place mostly in the shadows, turning the most ordinary of sets (the couple's home) into a surreal nightmare.

The movie exists as a series of highly sexualized visuals that center on Ryli's otherworldly beauty (highlighted to great effect in the notorious razor blade scene). The narrative is almost wordless, mimicking real life reduced to its most basic elements.

Though much of the film could have been duplicated back in the 1920s, what is unique to its time is the homemade sex tape the couple watches. Their enjoyment of watching themselves romp flips on its head; at the end, Ryli is watching it alone. Mark made this film before the cre-

Mark and his *Despair* co-star, Bonzai. Photo: Baranowski Archive.

ation of Facebook, but he asks a question that is only becoming more important as time passes: do we continue to exist because our image does?

Query anyone who has ever tried to delete a profile on social media, and they are likely to answer "yes."

Filled with a sense of ritual, bolstered by a bleak soundtrack (where the keyboards take on the sense of a mind unraveling), *Despair* was a fine way for Mark and Ryli to announce, "We're here."

MB: We're all hustlers. Each of us has something to sell, whether our own goods or someone else's. I learned this at a young age, and I determined then that I would never be happy selling anyone's goods but my own.

Life happens, however, and to this day, the fruits of my creative labor—books, movies, music and art—have yet to accumulate to the point where I can finally shake loose of the "day job" as a locksmith in the commercial door industry. Fortunately, I've been in that position long enough to say I almost enjoy it.

That's the ultimate goal (for most), after all; making a comfortable living doing what you love. Whether you're single or married, with children or without, it takes money to survive. It also takes money to make

Locksmith by day.... Photo: Baranowski Archive.

money, and yes, money does indeed buy happiness. Shame, not enjoying what you do to make it.

As an artist, I've strove for years to turn my hobby into my job. Again, that's yet to happen, but I've at least come close by doing one thing, in particular... making movies.

Say "I make movies" to someone and you'll either be met with looks of doubt, raised eyebrows, or an assuming smirk. Here in Charlotte, North Carolina—part of the Bible Belt—the smirk is most common; people immediately assume you're making pornography. Throughout my first ten years as an independent filmmaker, I was unfairly labeled "Porn King," and not so unfairly referred to as "Mister Nude" (the latter coming from someone who had actually watched my films). I have nothing against pornography, and perhaps some of our material walks the line between soft and hardcore, but I don't appreciate being judged based on assumptions.

Back in late September 2001, I was blissfully oblivious to any of this. While the United States was still reeling from the events of 9/11, my wife, Teresa, and I were living in a minuscule apartment. I was out of a job, and the bills were piling up. Teresa was working to support us both while I focused on drawing and writing. Over in Los Angeles, my manager was pitching my latest spec screenplay, *A Dangerous Motive*, which I'd written specifically for Jean-Claude Van Damme (my idol) to play the lead. Unfortunately, Van Damme was no longer a "hot property" in Hollywood, so it was instead being offered to the likes of John Travolta, Nicholas Cage, and Ray Liotta. Or so I was told....

My manager would say, "The wheels turn slowly out here," and insisted I remain patient on the east coast while she continued looking for someone to buy my script on the west. Meanwhile, I had just completed another, a sequel to John Carpenter's 1982 film, *The Thing*. This time referring to my copy of the Hollywood Creative Directory (I'd used the Hollywood Agents & Managers Directory to locate a manager), I began sending email upon email to potential buyers—including Universal Studios, who, unbeknownst to me then, still owned the rights to *The Thing*.

The amount of calls and emails I received in response to my *Thing* script was astounding. It seemed I was having better luck on my own than with a manager... until the cease and desist letter came from Universal Studios. They had no interest in reading my work, but they made sure no one else would, either.

So, what then? I needed to work, but again, I wanted my job to be something I truly enjoyed. A few months earlier, I'd contacted actor/producer/director Bruce Campbell, hoping he could help get my scripts into the right hands if he himself wasn't interested in reading them. His reply was, "Don't look to anyone else to fulfill your dreams. Become a producer and shoot the films yourself."

It was exciting enough just to hear back from him, even if it wasn't the response I was hoping for. I chose to ignore his advice at the time, having no knowledge of what it took to be a producer, much less to make a film. Besides, all I wanted to do was write films, not shoot them. By the time I received the letter from Universal, however, I was desperate to step outside of my comfort zone and make something happen.

I still knew very little about making movies, except that it requires people, money, equipment and at least one location. People... I had Teresa and myself. (Oh, and our miniature dwarf bunny, Bonzai. Not a person, but a talented actor, nonetheless.) Money... I had none. Equipment... I

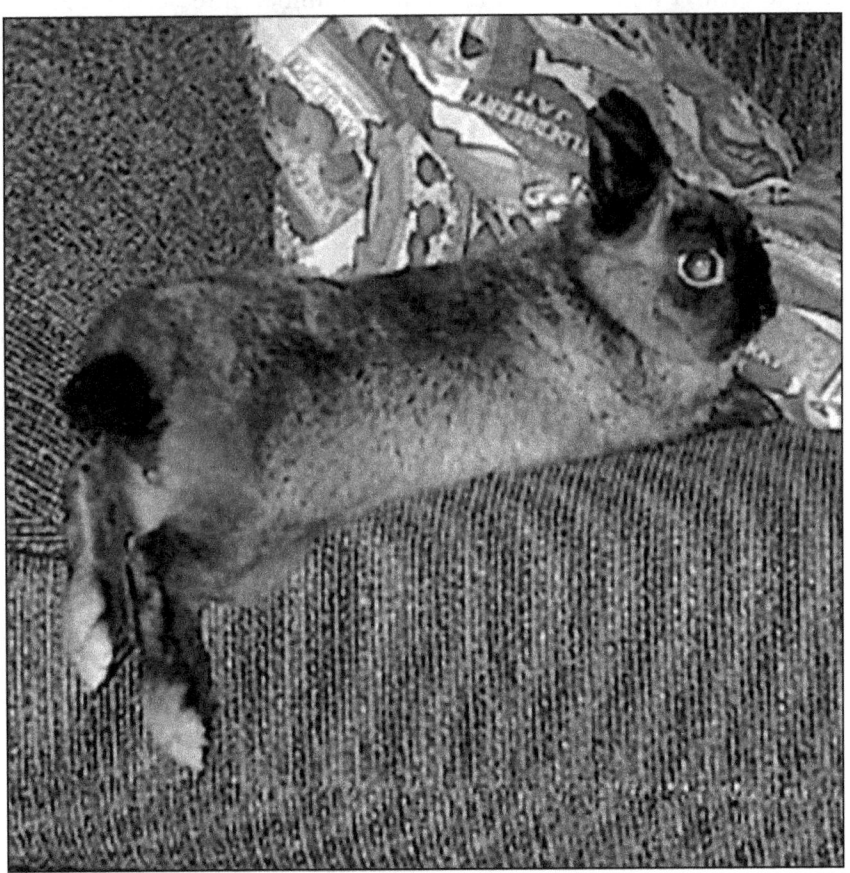

Bonzai! (R.I.P.) Photo: Baranowski Archive.

had the VHS-C camcorder that Teresa's parents had bought for her, some years back. Location… We were living in it. Herein lies the main lesson of this book, and the most important advice I could offer a budding filmmaker: *Work within your means.* If we hadn't, we never would have made it as far, or stayed as prolific, as we did for the next ten years.

Admittedly, I've always been a step behind when it comes to technology. I was still playing 8-track tapes and vinyl when audio cassettes were the rage, and the latter when CDs were the format of choice. Likewise with video, I refused to buy DVDs for the longest time because my movie collection already consisted of nearly 1,000 VHS cassettes. Now it's all about Blu-Ray… I don't care to know what comes next.

By late 2001, the average indie moviemaker was either shooting on film or digital video (DV). Consumer-grade cameras were mostly MiniDV, but you could still find VHS-C cassettes in your local Best Buy. True to form, I went the latter route, for a number of reasons: we already had a working camera; I had neither the money to buy, nor the time to learn, a new one; and I could care less about camera specifications. I believed then, and still do, that it's not about what you shoot with. It's about what you're shooting.

Needless to say, I wasn't going into this with any intention of having my work screened in theaters, or even film festivals. Whether another company distributed our films or we did so ourselves, I've always been perfectly content with creating "straight-to-video" material.

Which brings me to *Despair*, our first film. Once Teresa had left for work that late September morning, I spent the day putting pen to paper. By the time she got home, I'd finished writing the first draft of the script. The story was one of art imitating life—Teresa's and mine—only taken to grim extremes. Good or bad, it would certainly get people's attention.

My main cinematic influence for the project was Jorg Buttgereit's *Der Todesking (The Death King)* (1990), which I enjoyed a great deal more so than his earlier, better-known grue-fest, *Nekromantik* (1988). In creating the shooting script—my first—for *Despair*, I took a closer look at Buttgereit's film; specifically, shot composition and angles. This would not only help me determine how to present the similar imagery of *Despair*, it would also provide the basis for my later directorial decisions.

Once Teresa had returned home from work the following day, the shooting script was ready—and so was I. Teresa had no sooner put down her purse than I had camera in hand, telling her to shed her clothes and get to her knees for the opening shot. Inconsiderate and selfish, I know…

Ryli prepares to embark on her downward spiral. Photo: Baranowski Archive.

My obsession had already begun. At least there was little dialogue for her to memorize.

The shoot went on for four hours, and then for another four, the next night, and… that was a wrap on our thirty-five-minute short film. It would be the first and last time that everything would play out as it was written, with no compromises or setbacks. The main challenge, of course, was remaining upbeat and positive behind the camera when, every few minutes, we'd have to step in front of it and act suicidal.

There were technical challenges, as well, due to the VHS-C format I'd insisted on utilizing. Although I was able to edit in-camera throughout the shoot, I would still need to score the film, add titles and transfer it all to a VHS cassette for duplication. Teresa already had the cassette adapter to convert VHS-C to VHS, and I had the musical equipment and two VCRs to handle both the score and video transfer. (It would be another two years before I upgraded my computer and got acquainted with non-linear editing.) I ordered an inexpensive titling machine that provided simplistic text to clinch the 1980s look I was going for, and within a week, I had my VHS master tape.

Despair. Photo: Baranowski Archive.

The only remaining task (my favorite, as it turned out) was to design the video box cover artwork. I chose to keep the design simple yet effective by featuring the film's most striking image—Teresa pulling a bloody razor blade from her mouth—along with the tagline, "When Death is the Greatest Reward." Then came the decision of whether Teresa should be credited with her legal name or the pseudonym she'd already created for her part-time modeling work, Ryli Morgan (which is how I'll address her for the remainder of this book). Because she's nude throughout *Despair*, she went with the latter out of respect for her family. Me, I'm too proud to use a fake name, no matter what I reveal on camera.

It would be that same pride that led us to be called On Mark Productions. I can't take credit for the name, however. Back when a friend and I were self-distributing our music, back in our hometown of Buffalo, New York, we did so as Nickel City Records. When I moved to Charlotte and that partnership dissolved, it was he who suggested I continue as On Mark Productions. Four years later, I was finally taking his advice as I put the finishing touches on the box cover art for *Despair*.

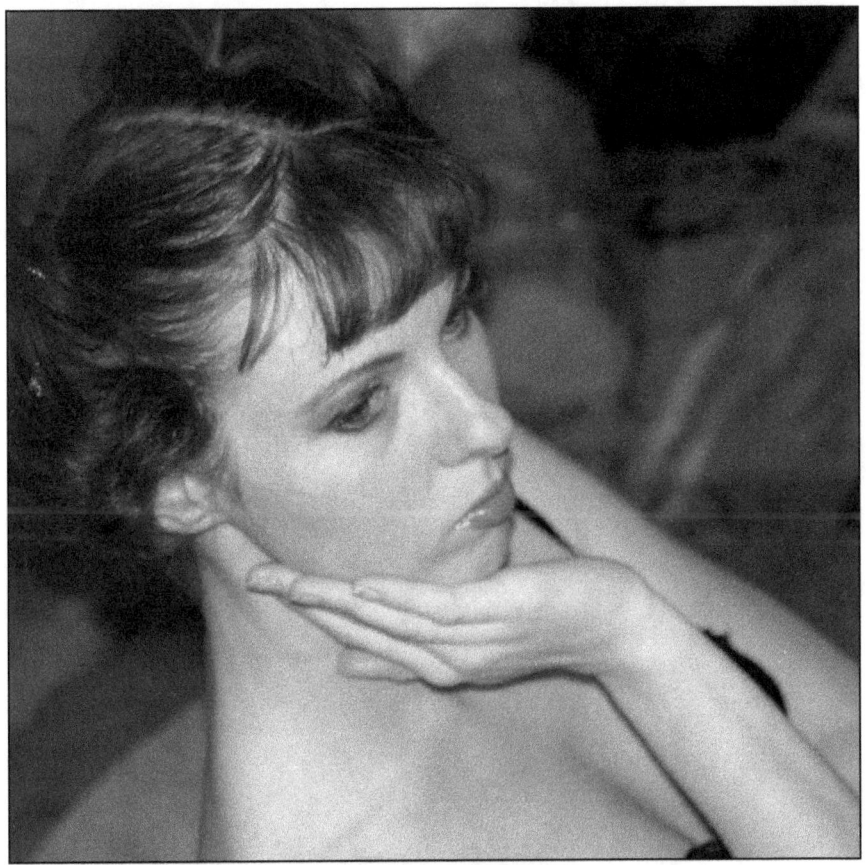

Ryli's early modeling days (2001). Photo courtesy of Kelly Kole/Baranowski Archive.

With that final task completed, I began running off copies of the video, while spreading the word about our first movie and taking orders from friends and family. Just as we relied on no one but ourselves in creating the film, I would ask no one for money when it came time to duplicate it. With a shopping list consisting of ink cartridges, printer paper, blank video cassettes, empty clam-shell videocassette boxes and cassette labels, my credit card balance(s) gradually began to rise.

Just as my debt continued its gradual ascent, sales were rising on account of a favorable review by famed film critic Joe Bob Briggs, and we were moving copies of the film just as quickly as we were piling them. I contacted a contributing writer for a local film zine, *Reel Carolina*, who offered to interview Ryli and I for the next issue. This meeting alone turned out to be a great product mover....

The interview took place at a bar in Charlotte's arts district, where the cast and crew from another independent production happened to be meeting to discuss their next scheduled day of filming. I gave David, our interviewer, a copy of *Despair*. It soon made its way to the bartender, who eagerly slid it into a VCR and, with no questions asked, screened the film on the television behind the bar.

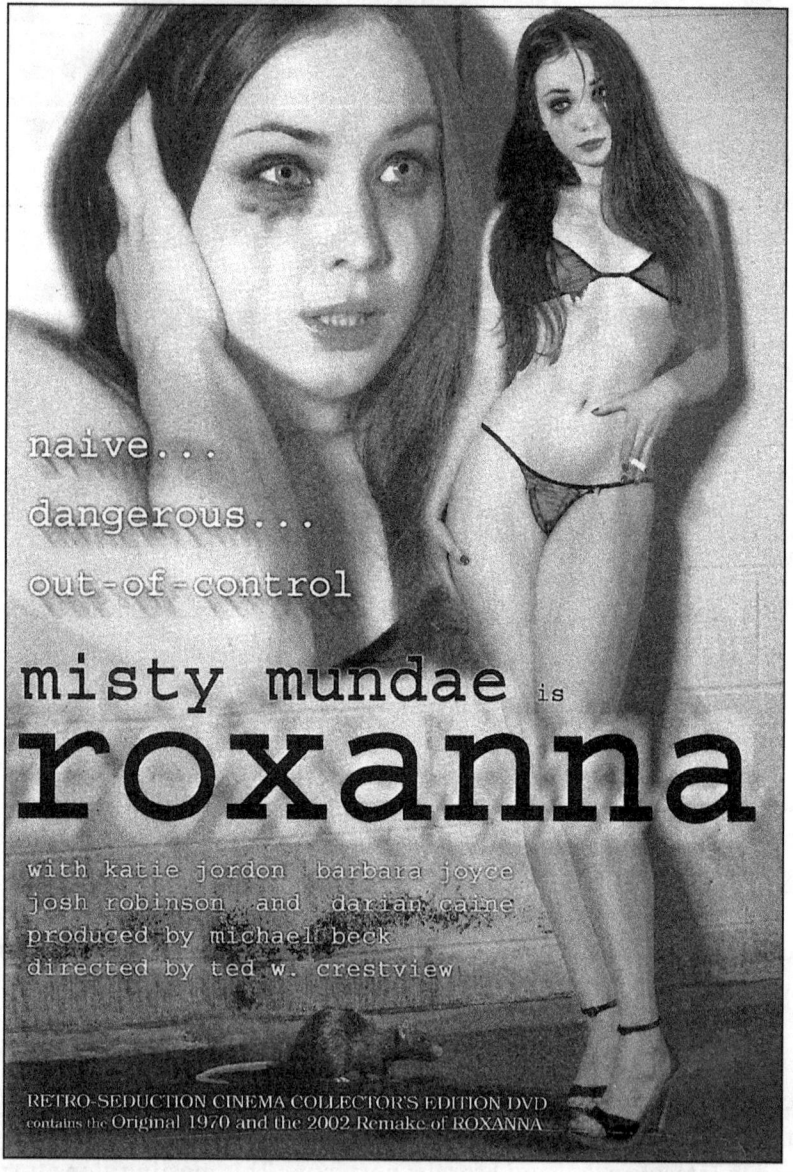

Roxanna DVD cover. Photo courtesy of E.I. Independent/ Seduction Cinema

If nothing else, the amount of nudity on display—both Ryli's and my own—was enough to appeal to everyone present. Men gazed from the Ryli that was naked on the screen to the fully clothed one at the bar, while women inched their way closer to me and remarked approvingly during my nude scene, "Nice butt!"

Although the compliments were greatly appreciated, I couldn't shake the nervousness about our impromptu film premiere being held in a public bar. *Hardly the time or place*, I thought. In any case, as the film ended, Ryli and I received a standing ovation. Orders for the film were immediately placed. Phone numbers were exchanged, along with numerous handshakes and hugs. David asked me to describe *Despair* in ten words or less. I couldn't… By that point, I was too excited to think.

From there, every trip to Blockbuster Video, Best Buy and Media Play meant adding to my list of potential distributors, compiled simply from reading the box covers of new releases. I contacted every company specializing in material similar to *Despair*, and within two months of its initial release, I was on the phone with Michael Raso at E.I. Independent Cinema. We worked out a deal, and just a few months later, our film could be found (if you looked closely enough) on video store shelves worldwide, featured among the bonus materials of E.I.'s *Roxanna* DVD.

And so it began….

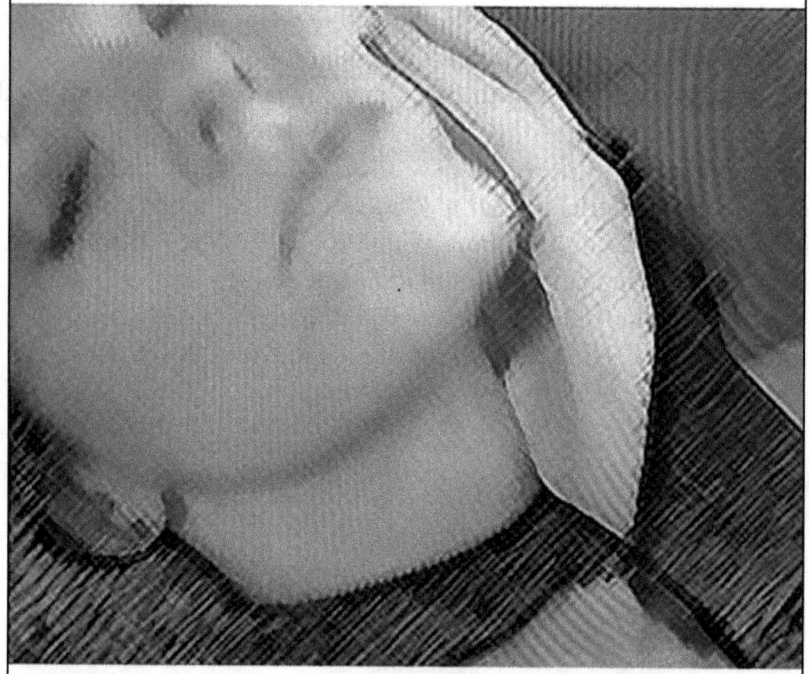

VHS box cover art. Photo: Baranowski Archive.

2

Ryli Morgan: Audition

Release date: February 7, 2002
Director: Everette Hartsoe
Producer: Mark Baranowski
Music: MARQUIS (Mark Baranowski)
Genre: Erotic, Adult
Runtime: 28 minutes
Cast: Ryli Morgan
Plot: *Ryli Morgan: Audition* showcases this rising model-actress at her stripteasing best! Directed and digitally recorded in September 2001 by Everette Hartsoe (*Razor*; *Vampire Call Girls*), in front of a blue screen and between the ropes of a boxing ring (!), Ryli sizzles while she struts, strips, sways and so much more… just for you! Watch, mesmerized, as she slides and wiggles out of three tantalizing outfits—each time more revealing than the last! If you you've been longing to see Ryli Morgan "in action"… *Ryli Morgan: Audition* delivers!

MB: Shortly after the completion of *Despair*, we met *Razor* comic book creator, Everette Hartsoe. Since becoming temporarily disenchanted with comics for financial reasons, Everette turned his attention to exploitation films. After discovering some of Ryli's modeling work online (she'd done several photo shoots within the previous year), he contacted her to request that she audition for an upcoming production.

The rendezvous took place at the offices of AEBN (Adult Entertainment Broadcast Network), a company in Charlotte that specializes in streaming porn videos on demand. They had their own studio, complete with a boxing ring, where daily shoots for their own *All Nude Sports* took place. It turned out that Everette was hired as lead writer/director for the show, which simply involved women undressing as they read the latest sports news, and that was the production Ryli was to audition for.

All her life, Ryli's been completely comfortable in front of the camera. Although this audition required her to perform a striptease—her first—and get fully naked in front of several people, she remained unfazed. Granted, she shimmied a bit too quickly through her striptease number at the start, but she soon found her groove and slowed things down quite nicely. By the time she'd climbed into the boxing ring, shed her snakeskin pants and towered over the camera in nothing but high heels, it was clear she was truly *All Nude Sports* material, and then some.

My idea of using that footage to create *Ryli Morgan: Audition* wouldn't come until months later, following Ryli's stint as an *All Nude Sports* reporter. She was still working for AEBN, but by then they'd moved

Ryli Morgan: Audition. Photo: Baranowski Archive.

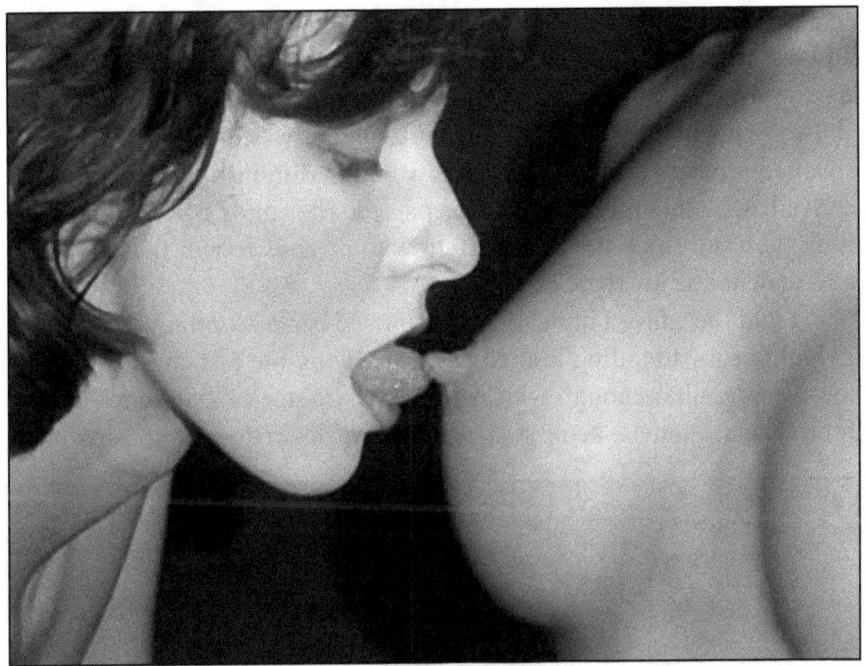

Ryli at work. Photo courtesy of AEBN/Baranowski Archive.

from news to comedic shorts, which Everette had written himself into. That was good news for him, as this allowed his off-screen cavorting with the staff lovelies to move in front of the camera, but bad news for AEBN's unsuspecting viewers. The remainder of the show's material forced the girls to act out their bisexual interests while exploring each other at great length.

Everette himself managed to get me hired on as a co-writer for the show, but never communicated to me what story lines had already been established, nor what direction to take. My workspace, which I shared alongside a chain-smoking editor, was minuscule and dimly lit. When Ryli wasn't working on-camera, she was either helping the other girls or researching material at a computer near enough to my desk where I could see the CEO frequently stopping by to offer her shoulder massages. Between his flirtatiousness and Everette's lechery, she could barely focus on her work. When she refused to provide Everette with sexual "favors," she was let go.

Her consolation prize was the master tape of her audition, which Everette had been promising us for weeks. Although I was happy to finally have that in hand, along with full control to use the footage as we so desired, I was outraged by the raw deal, not to mention the way Ryli—and our marriage—had been blatantly disrespected. Bright and early the next morning, I stormed through the doors of AEBN, fully prepared for a showdown with Everette and the CEO. Neither was in the office. Pacing, I waited anxiously, hoping my rage wouldn't diminish by the time they arrived. Minutes and more minutes passed. The editor stationed near my desk then informed me that Everette had errands to run that morning, and may not be in. The CEO was MIA.

I told the editor I quit, and never looked back. Months later, Ryli and I would begin attending film conventions along the east coast. Although few were familiar enough with AEBN to share stories, everyone—artists, filmmakers, models, actresses—with whom Everette had crossed paths

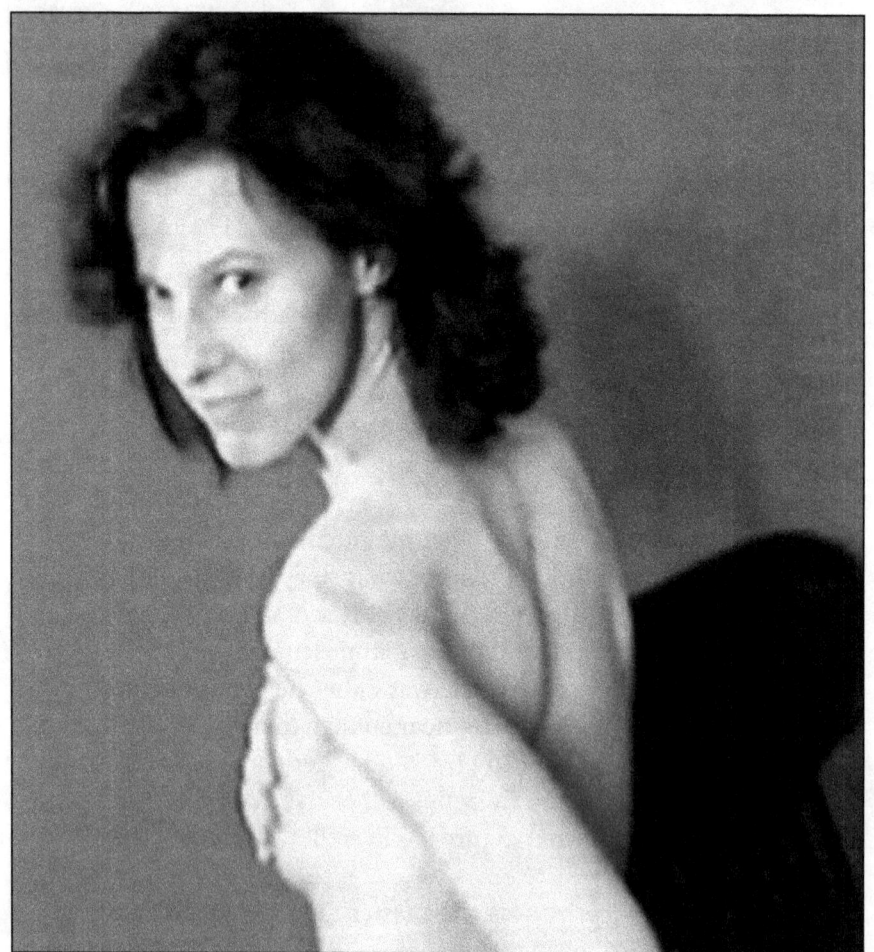

Ryli Morgan: Audition. Photo: Baranowski Archive.

stressed that the experience ranked high among the worst of their career. If only we'd met these folks sooner.

At least some good came from our "Everette experience"... *Ryli Morgan: Audition* soon became our second production, for which I was at least spared the tasks of directing and shooting. I edited, scored and packaged the film just as I had *Despair*, sold copies of both via my website, and wasted no time getting started on our next project.

VHS box cover art. Photo: Baranowski Archive.

3

Runaway Terror

Release date: June 14, 2002
Director: Mark Baranowski
Writer: Mark Baranowski
Producer: Mark Baranowski
Music: MARQUIS (Mark Baranowski), Dubok
Genre: Crime, Horror, Mystery, Thriller
Runtime: 72 minutes
Cast: Ryli Morgan, Melanie Murdock, Jami Harrelson, Mark Baranowski, Michelle Martin, Victoria Brigman, Jason Harrelson, Phyllis Barnette
Plot: A shady producer begins losing his actresses to a knife-wielding, masked killer. A detective teams up with the twin sister of the first victim to search for the culprit, as both the list of suspects and the body count grows.

SKB: Every fledgling filmmaker with dreams of working in horror has considered doing a slasher film. They have three distinct advantages: they don't require expensive special effects; they are based in a reality that we all understand (there really are scary people out there who commit these kinds of heinous crimes); and they operate on the simple good guy-bad guy formula.

Mark and Ryli certainly got ambitious with their slasher film, utilizing multiple locations (instead of setting the whole thing in a single house), and creating a plot with several twists. Once again, sex tapes play a certain role in the proceedings. (That was America in the early 2000s; if we couldn't watch ourselves doing it, it didn't happen.)

An intense moment. Photo: Baranowski Archive.

Mark had to juggle many hats—acting, producing and directing—and Ryli tackled not only production duties, but also had dual acting roles. Where *Despair* had an effective claustrophobic setting, Mark opened up *Runaway Terror*, displaying how no place is safe when a killer is on the loose.

The biggest drawback to movies depicting the aftermath of a murder is trying to cover the elements that an audience expects: detectives, police stations, and the nuts-and-bolts of an investigation. Here, Mark and Ryli try to play to their strengths and deflect the audience away from the fact that they can't show a long dolly shot of a working police station, or a team of cruisers screaming toward a crime scene. Instead, they focus on the relationships at the heart of the case. The simple camera setups force the audience to direct their attention to what's at the heart of the scene.

In this case, it's a cop who is getting entirely too cozy with the sister of a victim. Ryli becomes the special effect in these scenes, helping to cover for production problems that invariably crop up when you don't have the money to close down streets, hire pros for crew, and spend weeks in post-production for things like ADR (that's Automated Dialogue Replacement, for the casual reader).

Although Mark has said that this film was his biggest disappointment of his oeuvre, pay attention to what the writer/director/producer did when faced with these challenges: he adapted, persevered and completed. This isn't just a "when life gives you lemons" lesson. As a filmmaker, you have a responsibility to everyone involved. Whatever happens (short of your pulling a bonehead move that gets someone killed), finish the movie!

MB: At least a year before deciding to make our own films, I began a cross-country correspondence with Helen Haxton at Miklen Entertainment, a California production company specializing in erotic features. Following

Mark and Ryli on location. Photo: Baranowski Archive.

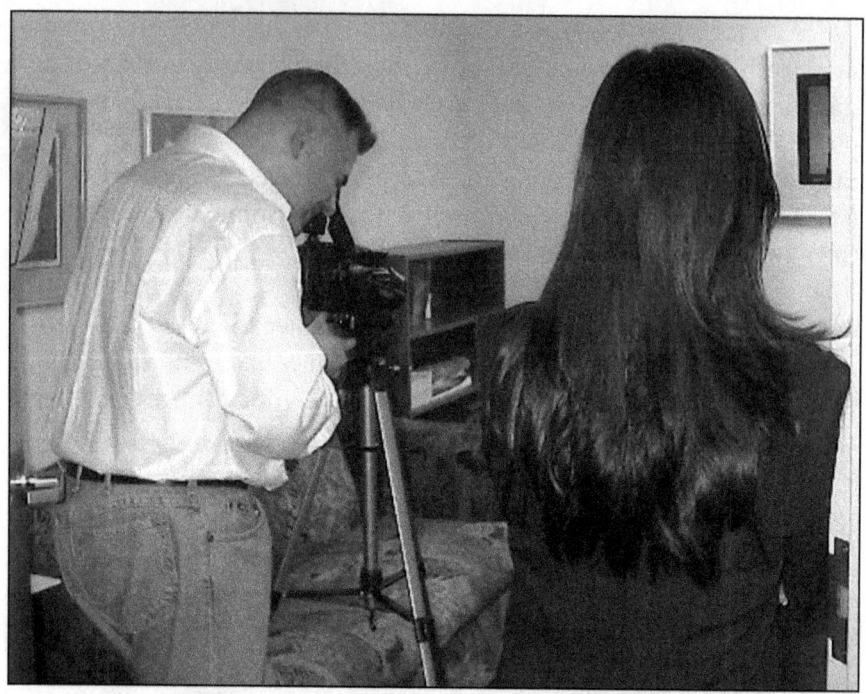

Mark, shootin' his shot. Photo: Baranowski Archive.

every possible lead into the industry as a screenwriter, I offered Helen my services. She was incredibly gracious, and provided tremendous feedback on a script I wrote for her consideration, initially called *Silent Partner*. (She said the title had to go; it wasn't "sexy" enough.) After a number of rewrites, however, Helen dropped out of touch, and the script ended up on a pile of similar dust collectors.

With *Ryli Morgan: Audition* completed and already selling quite well, *Silent Partner* was the first script that entered my mind when considering what our next production should be. I felt it could be made on a micro-budget such as ours, cast with friends excited by the mere fact that we were making movies. Never mind they had no acting experience… I believed (and, to an extent, still do) that enthusiasm alone would bring out a worthy performance. Besides, the "cattle call" element to the audition process is far too degrading and unnecessary for a low-budget movie. Business or not, it's important to keep both a level head and things in perspective.

I compiled a list of our closest friends, with a star next to those who'd exclaimed, "I want to be in your next movie!" The good news was that we had more names on the list than the script had characters. The bad news was that most of the female characters in the script had to get naked or be involved in a sex scene—alone or otherwise. Very few of our friends would be willing to disrobe for the camera, even if we paid them. It was time to get online and post our first casting calls.

We had no idea where to begin, and admittedly, we ended up looking for girls in all the wrong places: modeling websites; classifieds; message boards; strip clubs; Hooters restaurants; the cast of "All Nude Sports"... Those we approached in person either passed on the offer or laughed in our faces, as if we weren't actually making a movie (or a legitimate one, at least). Internet responses were just as discouraging, especially considering the only ladies willing to perform nude were located in states far beyond the Bible Belt.

This would prove to be the greatest thorn in our side, from then on. Although we weren't making porn, our Southern Baptist neighbors didn't see it that way. In this land of misconception, nudity itself was considered pornographic, and no argument would sway their way of thinking. It would be the only time I compromised, but for *Silent Partner*, I had no choice but to rewrite the script. Repeatedly.

Rather than have two actresses play sisters, for instance, the characters became twins. Ryli would play both. The original shower masturba-

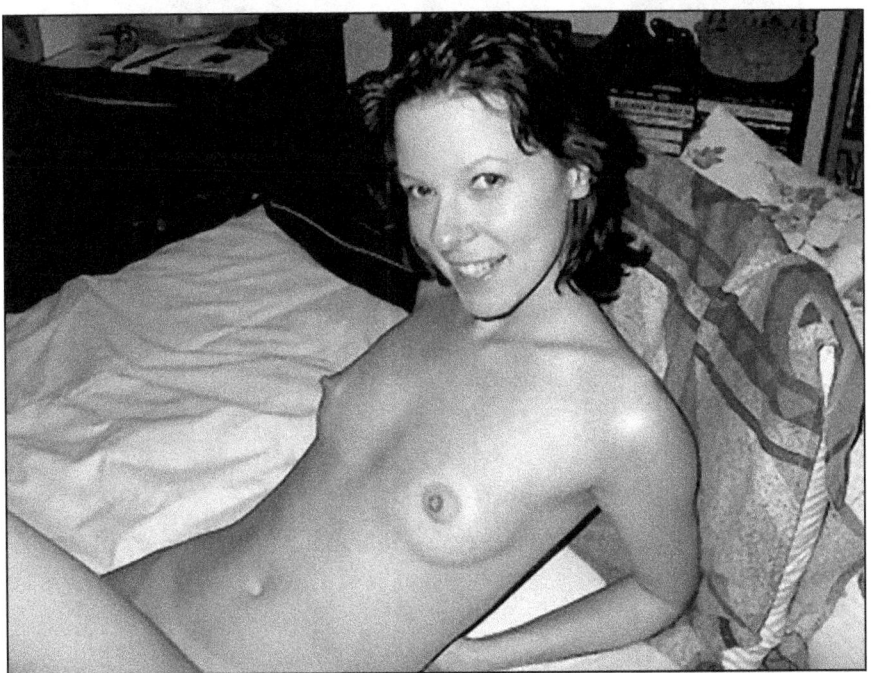

No shame in her game: Ryli happily bares all for Mark's loving camera.
Photo: Baranowski Archive.

tion scene instead left her with "the cleanest boobs in the business," as her mother would later remark. A close friend of ours from Cuyahoga Falls, Ohio was scheduled to play one of the supporting roles while on vacation at our place, until she backed out "for personal reasons" and skipped the vacation. A local actress who probably felt like she was slumming it quite nicely filled her shoes.

I'd recently been offered the locksmith position I left behind nine months earlier, and was now working part-time (a small help in throw-

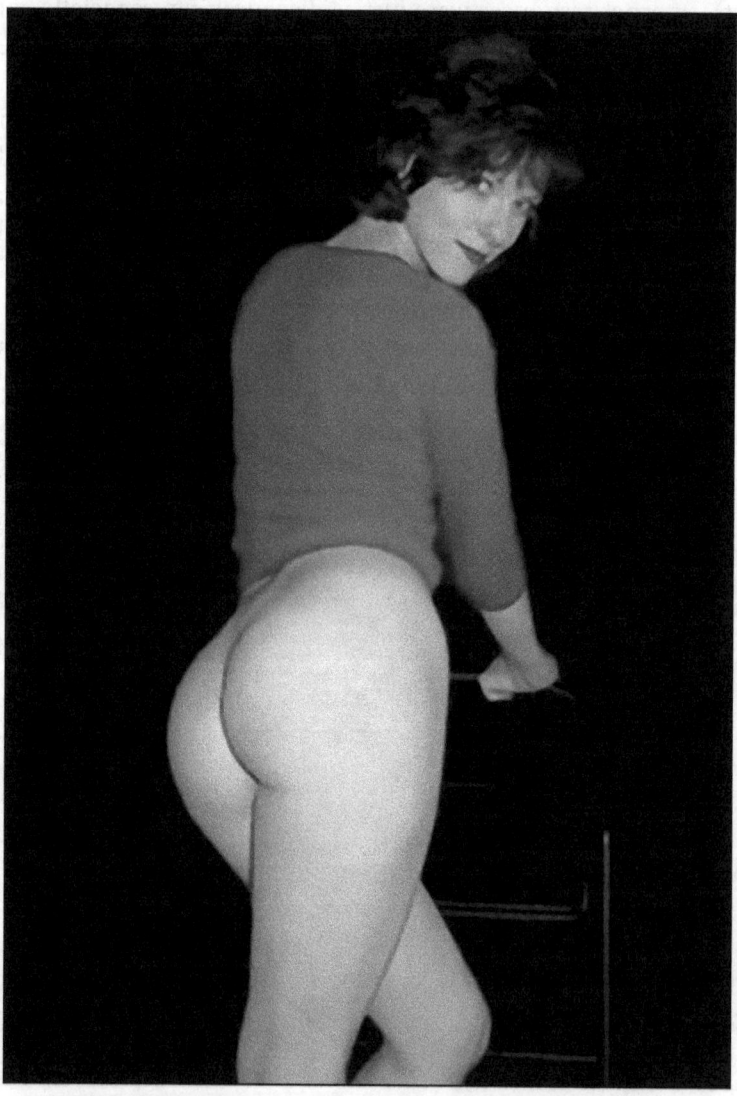

Ryli shares her "true Southern beauty" when posing for the *Runaway Terror* cover design. Photo: Baranowski Archive.

Leggy lovelies: Victoria Brigman and Melanie Murdock practice their dialogue.
Photo: Baranowski Archive.

ing money at my ever-increasing credit card debt). A major scene had to be rewritten after my boss yanked its first intended location out from under me. The shoot was to take place at my actual office, and would have lasted no more than a couple of hours. The boss's younger brother had happily allowed me to come in early on a Saturday morning just for this purpose. When the boss found out the night before, however, he decided to follow up on the rumors he'd been hearing about me—and the movies I was making—by visiting my website. Within minutes, he was dialing my number and criticizing my interests, the people I associated with, and the reputation I was getting at the office. He assured me I was going to hell, and that if my pursuits weren't "for the glory of God," I would never be blessed with success.

Naturally, I should have hung up the phone after the first minute, but because he was my boss and I feared for my job, I allowed his tirade to continue for nearly an hour. Once it was over, I asked him if all this meant that I wouldn't be allowed to shoot the scene the next morning. It did.

Fortunately, Ryli had just secured a temporary position, and was already comfortable enough with her supervisor to ask if we could shoot the scene there. A risky move, where her job was concerned, but we were granted permission and knocked out the scene as quickly as possible. Even one of Ryli's co-workers was cast (out of desperation). The bad news was that we didn't knock out the scene quickly enough. A shoot that would have lasted a couple of hours at my office dragged on for a couple of days at Ryli's.

I needed the additional time to get familiar with this new location. Besides, there were other people (i.e. noises) to contend with, and I'd assigned lines of dialogue to a girl who'd never acted before, nor shared my friends' enthusiasm for it.

A week or so later, Ryli lost her job.

Another bad decision on my part was using my father's house for a location while he was out of town. My relationship with him was still experiencing growing pains, and we weren't on speaking terms at the time. Nev-

Mark with Jami Harrelson, on location. Photo: Baranowski Archive.

Jami, all bloodied up and lovin' it! Photo: Baranowski Archive.

ertheless, since I knew where in the yard he kept the key hidden, I selfishly took advantage of the situation and brought several strangers into his house for the sake of my little movie. Nothing was taken, or even touched, but that certainly didn't make it okay. Of course, thanks to one of the neighbors, he found out. If he hadn't, I still wonder how long after we worked things out it would have taken me to tell him myself... or if I ever would.

At the halfway point of production, I was forced to substitute locations from what the script called for to whatever became available. Inclement weather and sudden conflicting schedules left me with no choice but to postpone weekend shoots. Continuity? Don't get me started....

Had I the patience to stick to the script or wait until it was convenient for everyone to proceed, the film may have turned out as it was originally written. Then again, it may never have gotten completed. I decided the latter was more likely, and I rewrote the last act to involve only Ryli's character(s), my own, and those of the friends/actors I knew I could count on. The result was far less grandiose, but at least it tied things up nicely.

There still remained the matter of changing the title to something catchier, if not sexy. Inspired by a radio spot for Lucio Fulci's 1981 film, *House by the Cemetery*, during which the commentator mentions a "runaway nightmare," I settled on *Runaway Terror*. Barely a descriptive of the

The not-so-scary truth: Plaid boxers and a glass of fake blood.
Photo: Baranowski Archive.

film itself, it actually refers to the film within the film. Although I've always been a fan of horror films, I had little interest in making them. When your budget's low, however, it's your best bet for finding an audience. (It would be another two years before that ceased to matter to me.)

This was to be the last time I relied on the VHS-C camera and two VCRs to complete a film, due in equal parts to how much of a hassle the process was, and because audiences surely wouldn't continue to overlook our technical limitations. Honestly, between its poor sound quality and desaturated color (necessary due to the multihued vertical line left by each cut), *Runaway Terror* is my greatest disappointment. Only its soundtrack, an equal selection of my own material and that of former Ohio-based electro band Dubok, holds it together.

Instead of a formal premiere, we simply invited cast members to our apartment for a viewing of the finished product. All seemed impressed and pleased with it, aside from their initial surprise by its lack of color. My shower scene (in extremely cold water, I must add; it's obvious) also raised a few eyebrows, as did my love scene with Ryli. Such was hardly the stuff of other local productions. Although this steamy material did little to affect the reputations of our friends, those with acting resumes now had *Runaway Terror* on theirs… whether they chose to acknowledge it or not.

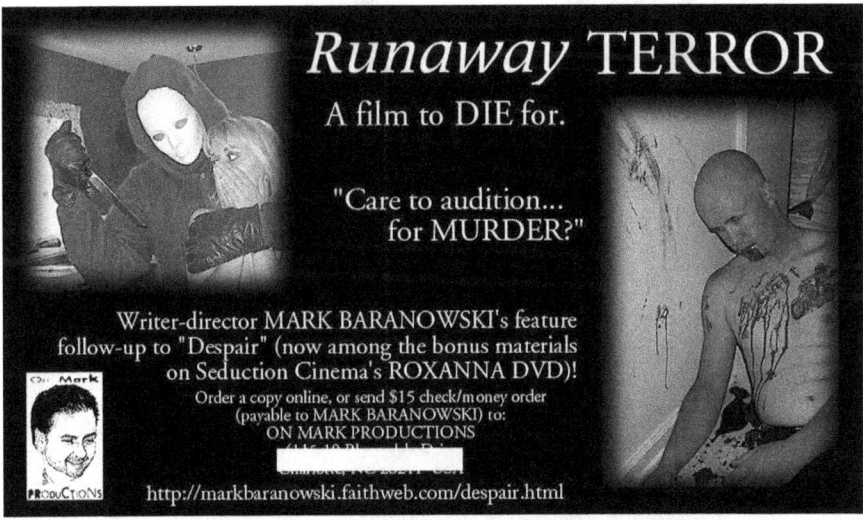

Ad design for *1313* magazine. Photo: Baranowski Archive.

Final poster design. Photo: Baranowski Archive.

Ad design for *Gothic Beauty* magazine. Photo: Baranowski Archive.

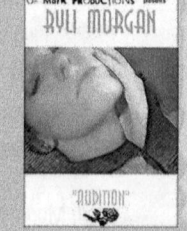

Full-page ad design for *Dr. Squid* zine. Photo: Baranowski Archive.

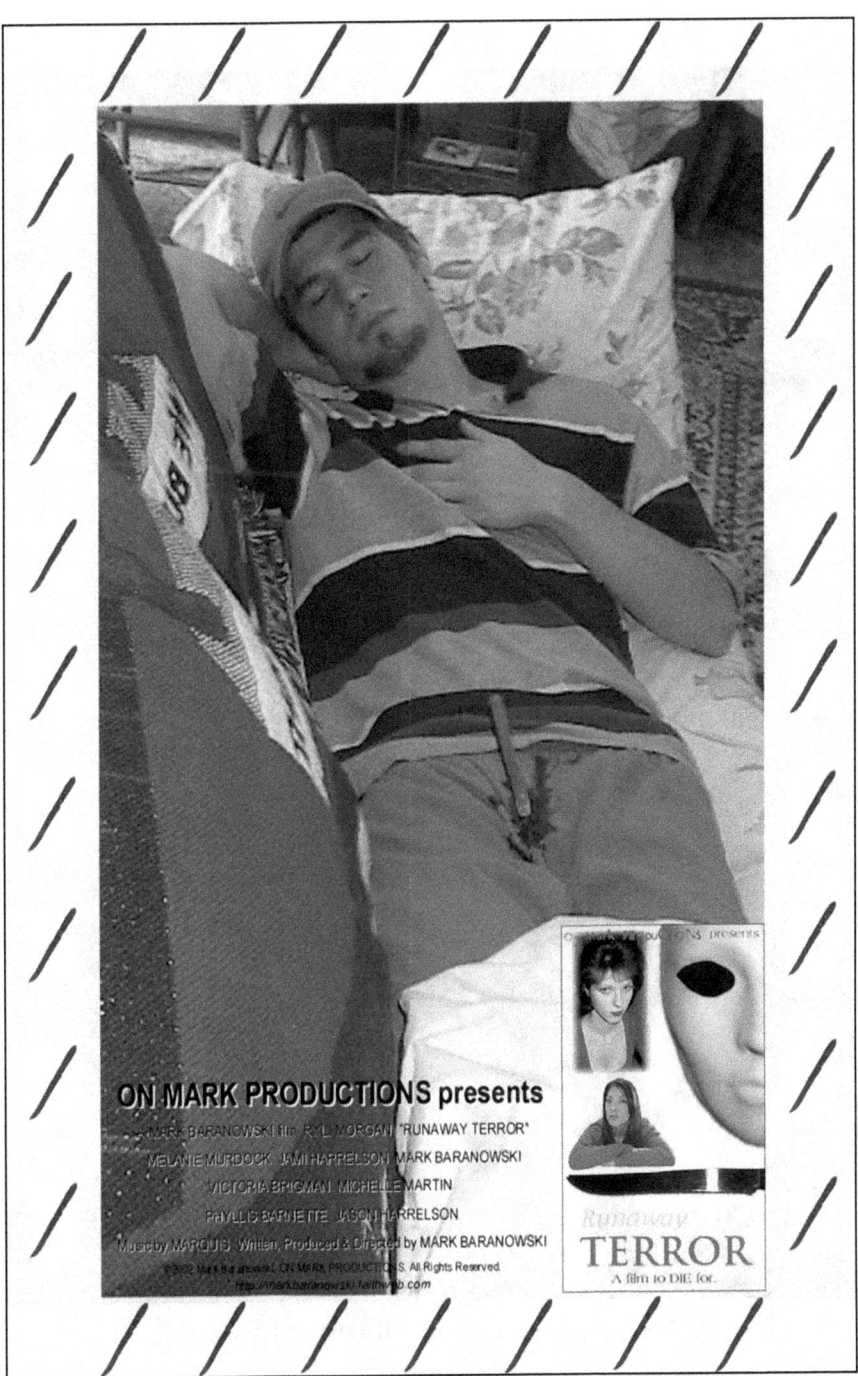

Unused poster design. Photo: Baranowski Archive.

Teaser poster design. Photo: Baranowski Archive.

4

The Zombie Room

Release date: UNRELEASED
Director: Mark Baranowski
Writer: Mark Baranowski (based on a story by Ryli Morgan)
Producer: Mark Baranowski
Music: MARQUIS (Mark Baranowski)
Genre: Horror
Runtime: ???
Cast: Ryli Morgan, Mark Baranowski, Jason Harrelson, Erin Greene, Michelle Martin, Jami Harrelson
Plot: Five friends head out to the country for the weekend and pick up a peculiar hitchhiker along the way. As night falls, their passenger's true identity is revealed, as he attacks the group, one by one.

MB: Still riding the wave of excitement from acting in *Runaway Terror*, a few of my friends (brothers Jami and Jason Harrelson, and Jami's girlfriend, Michelle) were anxious to go another round, a few months later. Naturally, so were Ryli and I—along with Erin, a pretty black girl Ryli worked with at her new job in a Neurosurgery office. I began writing what was to be our first all-out horror film, which I felt was important since we were becoming horror film convention regulars. With a title inspired by a Depeche Mode song and an original story idea from Ryli, *The Zombie Room* script was underway....

From Day One of this project, I spent more time promoting it than creating it. With only ten script pages written, I'd already designed a promotional ad for the film and paid for it to appear in the next issue of *Rue*

Five friends and a bloody stranger face a strange sight. Photo: Baranowski Archive.

Morgue magazine. I ordered the special contact lenses to be worn by our titular creature, along with plenty of makeup and stage blood. I bought a MiniDV camera and a computer well equipped for editing. There was a fair amount of talk, from zombie lovers especially, circulating about the film on the Internet. Our motivation couldn't have been stronger.

Bob, one of my co-workers, lived in New London, nearly an hour away from our home in Charlotte. He'd mentioned an abandoned, ramshackle house that was located about a mile from his own. It sounded perfect for *The Zombie Room*. Based on Bob's description of it, I wrote the house into my script and planned for the first Saturday shoot to take place there. I also worked with Jami and Jason, who lived together with Michelle, which made everything quite convenient. It was arranged that Erin would ride with us to Jami's, who would follow us to Bob's in his own car, accompanied by Jason and Michelle.

I met Erin for the first time when she arrived on the morning of the shoot. Nice enough, and just as excited about the film as the rest of us, she had me in high spirits as we drove toward Jami's apartment. Upon arriving, we found Jami and the gang almost ready to go, and actually eager to start the rather long and tedious trip out to Bob country. Within minutes, we hit the road.

Much of that road, NC-49 North, was a straight, single-lane stretch of pavement, sidelined by a steel rail to the right and thick woods to the

Ad design for *Rue Morgue* magazine. Photo: Baranowski Archive.

left. We'd driven at least twenty minutes without much conversation, so I turned on whatever CD I had in the stereo. I recall getting a bit too wrapped up in the music, and paid more attention to what we were passing than on the road ahead. The speed limit was 45 mph, and although there'd been a good bit of traffic in front of us, no one was tailgating (for a change).

Mark, Jami, and Ryli. Photo: Baranowski Archive.

I was probably doing about 52 mph when I looked from my right to the road. Everyone's taillights were suddenly shining, and we were approaching the car in front of us way too fast. I had no time to discover the reason, nor was there a shoulder at the right of the road to swerve onto. Instinctively, I swerved left—into oncoming traffic—and stepped on the gas. As we passed one car after another, I could see the first one in line was waiting to make a left turn as oncoming traffic approached. Miraculously, I managed to slip in front of that first car before it could turn, quite literally a second before colliding head-on with the oncoming vehicle.

None of us said a word during, or after, the incident. It all happened so quickly that I actually thought (hoped?) the girls hadn't even noticed. Their eyes had been closed earlier, after all… Maybe they'd snoozed through it. In any case, as much as I attempted to shrug off that near-

Jami gets reacquainted with "his" childhood home. Photo: Baranowski Archive.

death experience, my heart remained in my throat until we reached Bob's house.

The day's shoot went well enough, although the cold and misty March weather wasn't making the exterior scenes any easier. Only once did I attempt shooting the opening scene as it was written—with everyone but Ryli and I riding in the back of my pickup truck—but the wind wouldn't allow us to continue. With four people scowling at me miserably, their hair a mess, I had no choice but to borrow Bob's van for a re-shoot.

The passing traffic was another nuisance, since much of the opening scene takes place along the side of the road. Even with the new camera, I was concerned that the dialogue wouldn't be perfectly audible. Considering how great a distance we were from the city, the number of cars that went by once we started shooting was unbelievable. It began to appear that they were passing us only to catch a glimpse of a movie being made. I'm sure I saw the same cars several times.

As for the abandoned house, it truly was perfect. About fifty feet back from the road, trees surrounded it and there was no driveway. Its roof was still intact, but every window was broken. The front and back doors hung wide open. Inside, there remained little more than a useless television set, broken glass and chipped paint. I hadn't noticed it while first exploring, but Jami later pointed out a small, long-dead animal against the wall of what appeared to be the kitchen.

Once we began losing daylight, we packed up, returned Bob's van and headed back to Charlotte. I continued working on the script until the following Saturday, which was supposed to go according to the same plan. This time, however, Erin drove her own car and followed Ryli and I. Upon arriving at Jami's, we waited no less than ten minutes for someone to respond to our knocking at the door. Once it finally opened, we were greeted to a grimacing, half-awake (and half-dressed) Jami, who'd only been home from barhopping for about four hours.

The day's shoot started out as expected... Upon arriving at Bob's, Erin snapped at me for driving too fast for her to follow, and then Jami resented something I said about getting a late start and stormed off. It took some time, but once everyone calmed down, we got along well and became quite productive. Actually, we ended up with more bloopers than usable footage, but we enjoyed ourselves.

On our way home, we stopped at a restaurant for dinner. In hindsight, I should have picked up the bill, especially since Jami jokingly suggested it. Instead, I promised to do so once the film wrapped. Yes, I was a dick, and it made for an awkward moment, to say the least. Still, Jami was willing to shoot some additional footage for a teaser trailer afterward, and everyone's spirits seemed high enough to continue on the following Saturday.

Ryli surveys the location. Photo: Baranowski Archive.

Little does Mark know, there's a dead animal beside the sink.
Photo: Baranowski Archive.

It wasn't meant to be. It rained for the next three consecutive weekends. By the fourth, none of us even cared to mention the project. I'd stopped working on the script, and to this day, it's only half complete. Although Ryli continued to work with Erin, I never saw her again. Jami and Jason moved on to other jobs, and Michelle soon ended up with a new boyfriend. Bob even informed me that the abandoned house was torn down some months after our last visit.

Such a shame, and a terrible waste.

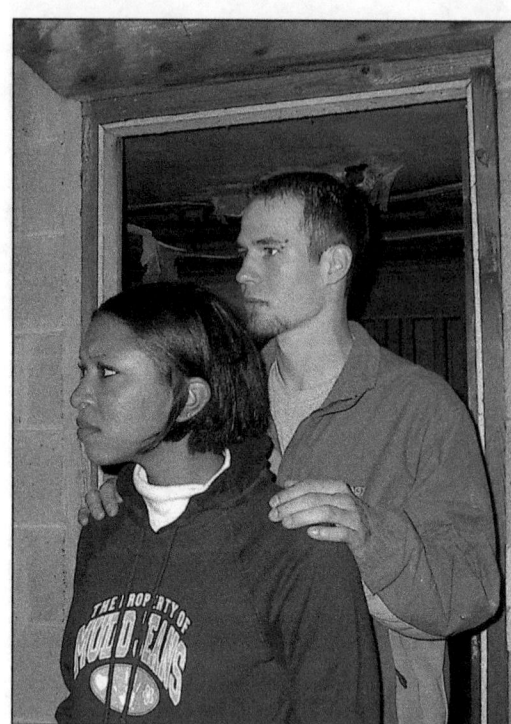

Erin and Jason get nervous.
Photo: Baranowski Archive.

Comin' at ya!
Photo: Baranowski Archive.

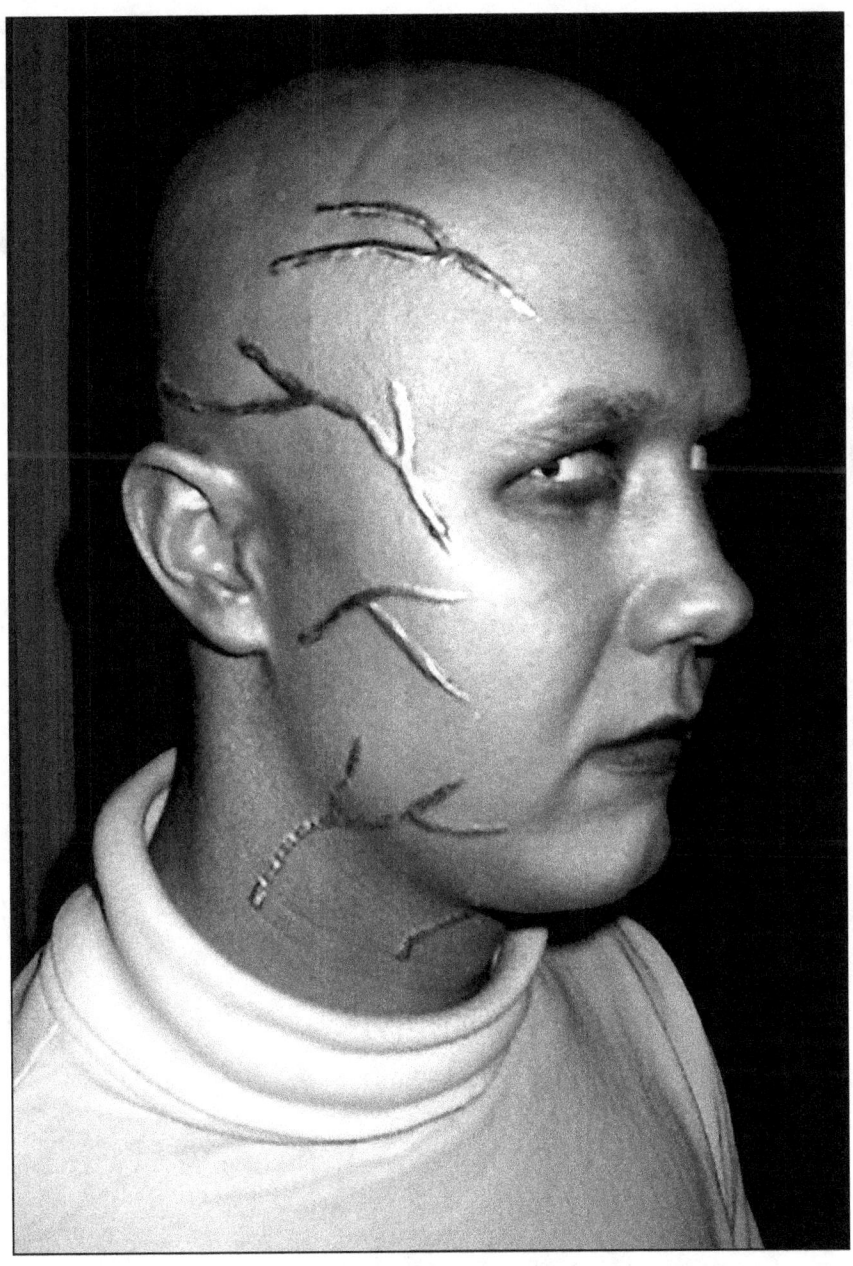
Jami in full makeup. Photo: Baranowski Archive.

Poster and DVD box cover art. Photo: Baranowski Archive.

4

Expendable

Release date: August 14, 2003
Director: Mark Baranowski
Writer: Mark Baranowski
Producers: Mark Baranowski, Ryli Morgan
Music: MARQUIS (Mark Baranowski)
Genre: Drama, Horror
Runtime: 56 minutes
Cast: Ryli Morgan, Mark Baranowski, Rachelle Williams, Brinke Stevens
Plot: David is a newly sold-out drug dealer who decides to pay his ex-wife, Nicole, a surprise visit before leaving town with his new girlfriend... only to discover that Nicole isn't the same person he knew when he left her, a year earlier. She now has a girlfriend of her own, and David soon realizes that some things are better left in the past.

SKB: Mark and Ryli were definitely hitting their stride by the time they made *Expendable*. Aside from being a thoroughly enjoyable (spoiler alert) vampire romp, it's notable for bringing a very blonde Ryli to the screen; introducing the world to Rachelle Williams (many a "thank you" are definitely in order); and having Brinke Stevens perform a dance that you still will be dreaming about when you're eighty and in a nursing home.

As befitting a vamp flick, this one borrows a page from Hammer and has a lesbian subtext that has probably been responsible for more than one trip to the emergency room with heart palpitations.

A still-delectable Brinke Stevens heats things up. Photo: Baranowski Archive.

Up to this point, Mark has cast himself in roles where he is pretty much Joe Average, trying to get through another day. In *Expendable*, he is all barely controlled anger, annoyed at the guy on the other end of a drug deal, and seething about his ex-wife. He seems ready to either explode or implode... but he never gets the chance.

Women definitely wield the power in this film, and that's probably the biggest departure from what we usually see in micro-budget horror films. Instead of waiting for five minutes before the end credits and seeing a frightened and abused woman kill to protect herself, the catch here is that the women are in charge from the get-go. Mark's character doesn't see it, but we know the minute we glimpse Ryli and Rachelle (and Brinke, too) that they are running the show. Men are definitely a bottom link on the food chain—in more ways than one.

There's an interesting inversion, too, in the settings. *Expendable* takes things back to the basics, with most of the action occurring in one house. The brilliance of it is that we don't notice. Watch the scene where Ryli is seated outdoors in her sunglasses and talking to Mark; you are blissfully unaware that they have just moved a few feet from the last location.

Ryli sees Mark's point. Photo: Baranowski Archive.

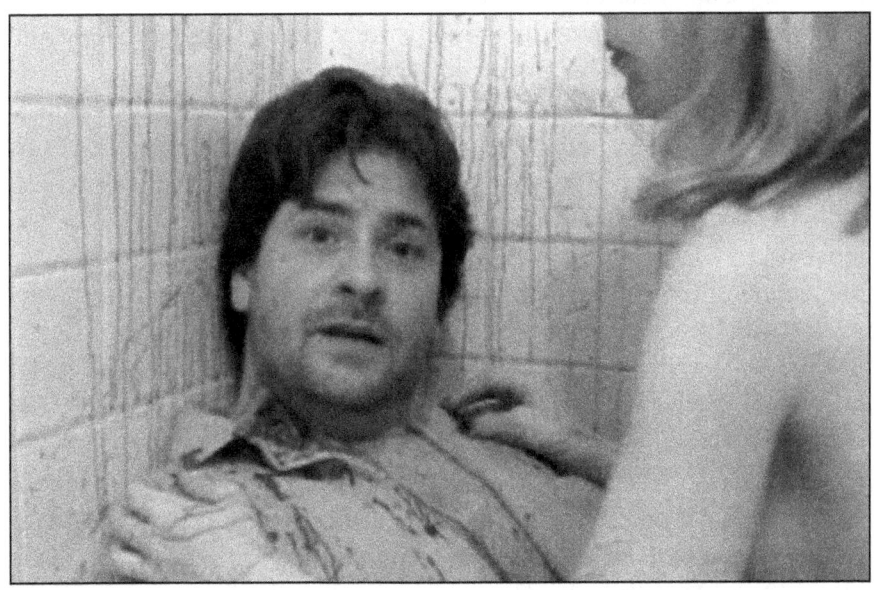

Bloody provocative, indeed! Photo: Baranowski Archive.

Ryli vs. Mark. Photo: Baranowski Archive.

One of the things that Mark intrinsically realizes as a filmmaker is what Arnold Schwarzenegger movies knew in the 1980s—if you have a big-ass gun, show the big-ass gun. In his case, he keeps the lens pointed at Ryli and all the background details seem to fade away. Nowhere is this more true than the film's ending, which probably could have run for about forty-five minutes and no fan would ever complain.

MB: By this time (Summer 2003), Ryli and I had moved out of our tiny apartment and into her parents' house. No longer burdened with rent or utility bills, the plan was to pay off our debts as quickly as possible and move on to a larger place (whether apartment or house) of our own. As the tagline of our next film would read, however, some plans just never work out right.

Shortly after leaving *The Zombie Room* behind, I wrote a new script that would involve only myself, Ryli, and two other females. I would shoot it at home, and on the streets of Charlotte… In other words, there would be no friends to rely on, and no hour-long drive to a location. I was confident that E.I. would distribute it as they had *Despair*, since it combined several key ingredients of their best-selling titles to form the perfect pitch: LESBIAN VAMPIRES GET NAKED AND BLOODY!

Draculina, a magazine covering B-Movies (and uncovering the actresses who star in them), had recently featured *Despair* in a column penned by a master wordsmith named Scott Barker. It would be Scott

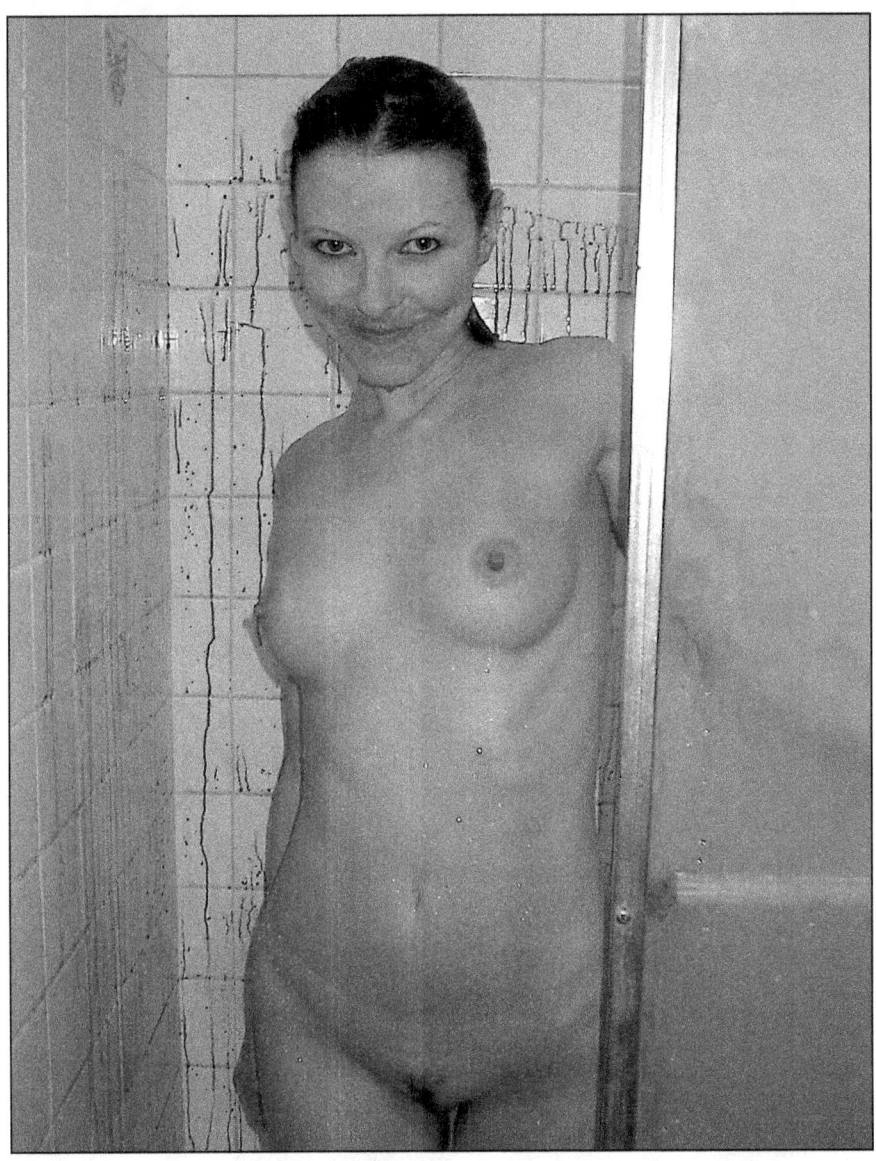

Ryli: "Care to join me?" Photo: Baranowski Archive.

who suggested we contact a certain young lady friend of his in Canton, Ohio, about playing one of the two remaining female characters in the film. I wasted no time doing just that, and she wasted even less in getting back to me with keen interest. I sent her the script, and in almost no time at all, she was on board. Her name was Rhonda, but she would ask to be credited as Rachelle Williams.

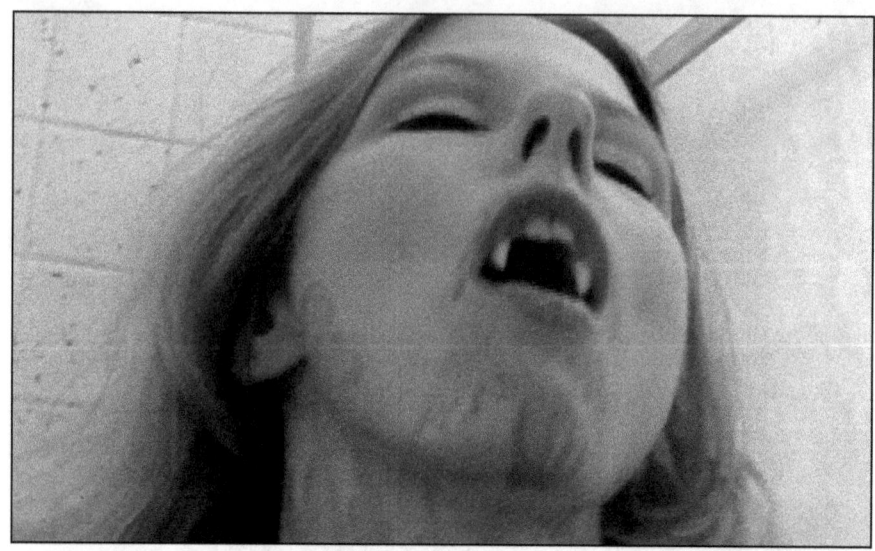

Ryli, in the role she was born to play. Photo: Baranowski Archive.

For the last role, I felt it was time to add a more familiar name to our cast list (the first strike against our plan to quickly pay off our debts). I emailed the legendary 1980s "Scream Queen," Brinke Stevens, with a humble request that she consider being a part of *Expendable*. She read the script and, to my sheer delight, happily accepted. To save me from covering her travel and accommodation costs, she even suggested that her own cameraman shoot her scenes exactly as they were written, and she would promptly send me the footage. We had a deal.

Rachelle, giving great phone…. Photo: Baranowski Archive.

Beautiful Brinke. Photo: Baranowski Archive.

All went according to plan, which was a tremendous relief, considering the unfortunate turn of events while shooting *The Zombie Room*. Granted, the heated dialogue between Ryli's character and my own often made tensions rise between us, but this only enhanced our scenes. While the majority of my films resulted in a great amount of gag reel footage, there would be none at all from *Expendable*. The only light moments came from Ryli, when she discovered my erection while shooting her intimate scene with Rachelle.

Most refreshing was how comfortable Rachelle was to perform nude, especially considering this was her first film. Of all the local actresses who'd sent me headshots and resumes throughout the previous year, not a single one would agree to such a thing. This reinforced our thinking that perhaps we'd be better off moving out of the Bible Belt if we were to

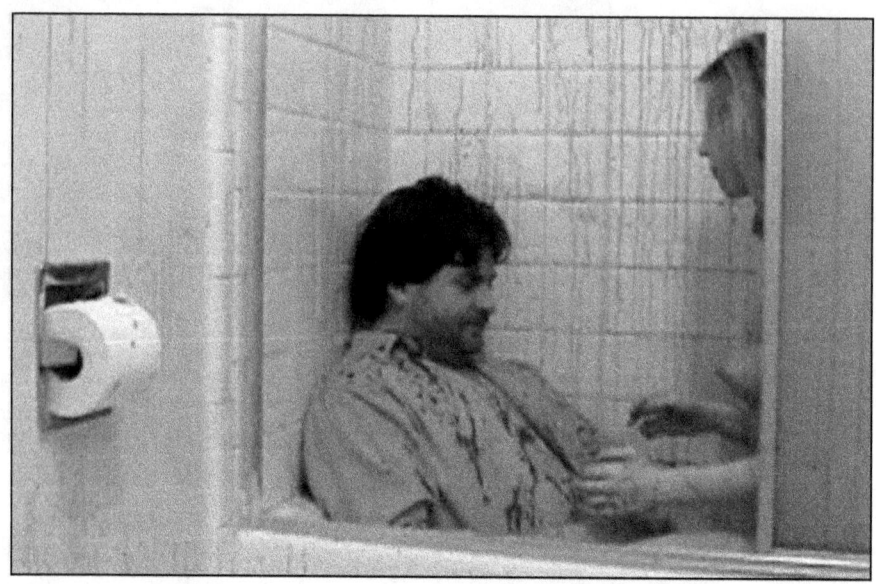

"If only this tub was wider...." Photo: Baranowski Archive.

continue making movies, but for the time being, I counted my blessings and swore to work with Rachelle as often as possible.

We took a tremendous risk, shooting the interior scenes at the front end of Ryli's parents' house while her mother busied herself at the back. The last thing we needed was for her to discover me in the bathroom, filming a naked Ryli and Rachelle as they French kissed and basted each other in fake blood. We even repainted the blood-splattered bathroom before Ryli's father arrived home from work, none the wiser. I took advantage of them for their house, just as I had of my father for his. Still inconsiderate and selfish, my obsession continued to grow.

Nearing the end of production, Ryli and I traveled through Charlotte one evening to shoot the reminder of exterior location footage we needed. Stopping on a whim at a small playground, I got out of my truck and began setting up my camera for the sake of no more than two static shots. Before I could push the Record button, a car pulled up beside me and a black man stepped out, claiming to be a member of the neighborhood Homeowners Association. Scolding us for being on "private property," he demanded I state our business there, and then ran us off with a story about trespassers recently littering the playground with empty beer bottles and used condoms. As we drove off, he glared at us as if we were the culprits.

From there, we went to get a single shot of a Pentecostal church, located just around the corner from Ryli's parents' house. I noticed two women

Boobs and blood? Rachelle's there! Photo: Baranowski Archive.

entering the building as we pulled into the parking lot, but I thought little of it until pulling to a stop at the far corner of the lot. I turned and found them still lingering in the doorway, watching us. After a few seconds, they went inside. Now feeling anxious, I tried my best to hurry as I brought out my tripod and camera. Once again, just as I was about to get the shot we were there for, a police car pulled into the driveway and parked behind us. The women had called the cops.

The officer was actually quite pleasant. I gave him one of my business cards, and he believed me when I told him the reason we were there. Of course, I didn't get the shot. Heading back home sullenly, I did a double take as we passed by the two women, still watching us from the doorway of the church. This time, it was me who glared.

Within the following week, I went elsewhere to get the exterior shots we needed, and that was a wrap. I'd become quite familiar with the new

Ryli and Rachelle get a little closer. Photo: Baranowski Archive.

computer and its pre-loaded editing program by then, and therefore, took what would become my average completion time for post-production duties: two weeks. Even with the "day job," my obsession with movie making wouldn't allow me to take things at a reasonable pace. I slept little, and thought of nothing but finishing the film. If I wasn't editing or scoring, I was miserable. If Ryli hadn't been so understanding and patient with me during these periods, our marriage surely would have ended on account of them.

Finally, *Expendable* was completed. I designed another promotional ad and spent hundreds of dollars for online and print advertising. Wheth-

Photo: Baranowski Archive.

er it was the film's subject matter or the fact that it featured Brinke Stevens, it sold tremendously. I literally spent no more than $5000 to make it, so we saw a profit within weeks. I utilized a website called CustomFlix (now CreateSpace) to distribute our films in DVD-R format, along with our usual VHS cassettes. After doing so with *Expendable*, I authored *Ryli Morgan: Audition* and *Runaway Terror* to a disc with some added bonus features. The satisfaction of having two fully packaged DVDs of our titles felt incredible.

Ironically, I never heard back from E.I. after sending them a screener copy of *Expendable*.

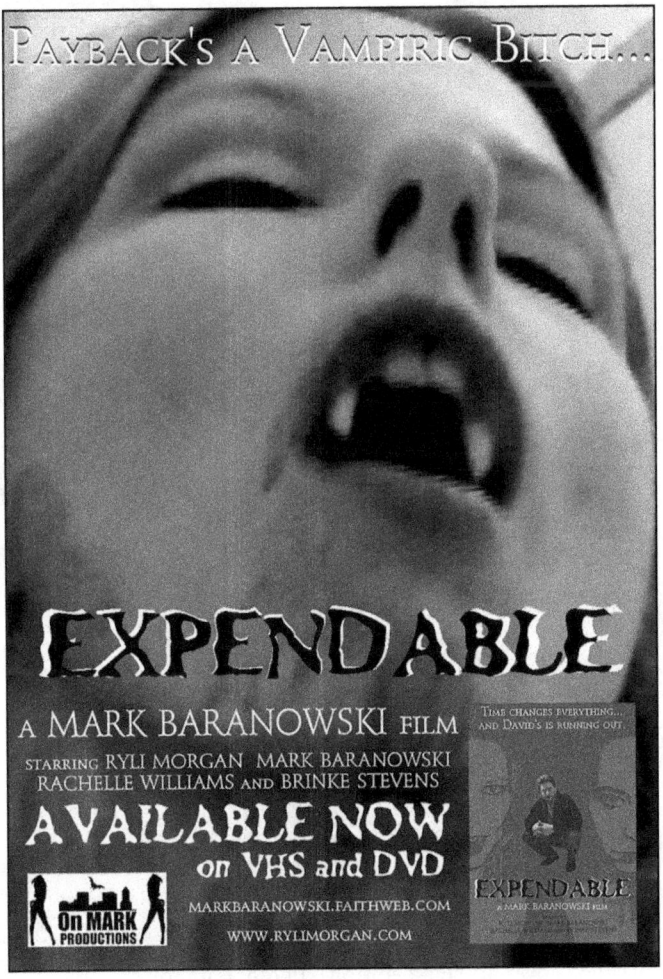

Ad design for *Rue Morgue* magazine.
Photo: Baranowski Archive.

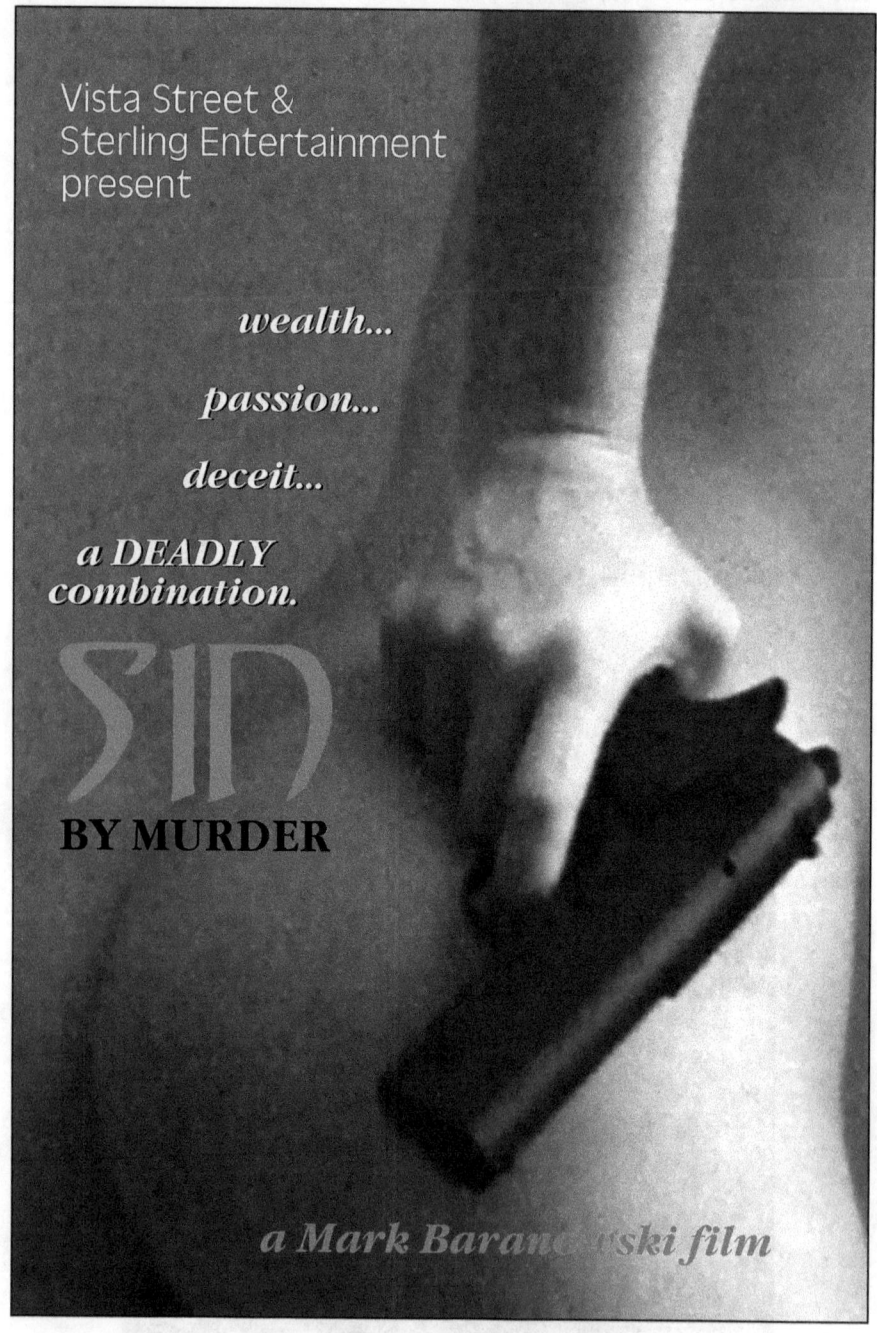

DVD box cover art (First edition). Photo: Baranowski Archive.

5

Sin By Murder

Release date: February 6, 2004
Director: Mark Baranowski
Writers: Stephen Downing, Mark Baranowski
Producers: Mark Baranowski, Ryli Morgan
Music: MARQUIS (Mark Baranowski), Ollie Olsen, False Profits Coalition
Genre: Erotic Thriller, Crime, Drama, Mystery
Runtime: 88 minutes
Cast: Tim Ross, Rachelle Williams, Jyllyan Dixon, Mark Baranowski, Ryli Morgan, Stephen Elliott, Michael Hicks, Jennifer Calhoun, Lauren Brower
Plot: On the night of their tenth anniversary, corporate lawyer Michael Barnes' wife is brutally murdered. Labeled the prime suspect by Detectives Jack Burns and Amy Cobb, Barnes must try to clear his name before it's too late. Along the way, Barnes' closest friends begin to show their true colors, and with no one left to trust, he finds himself with nothing to lose as he's faced with the toughest decision of his life.

SKB: Fish gotta swim, birds gotta fly, and filmmakers gotta stretch. It's a law.

Unless you're Michael Bay, in which case you can have a whole career of just blowing stuff up.

For Mark, that cinematic flexing can clearly be glimpsed in *Sin By Murder*, an ambitious thriller whose tagline could be (borrowing from Morrissey) "Marriage is Murder."

Tim gets horizontal with Rachelle.... Photo: Baranowski Archive.

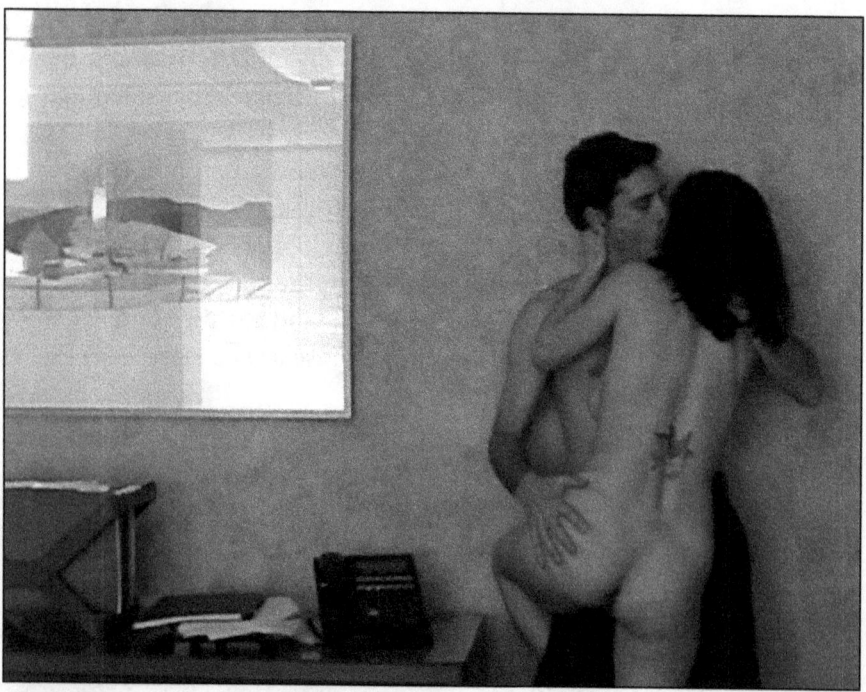
...but prefers to remain vertical with Jyllyan. Photo: Baranowski Archive.

The movie sets up Rachelle Williams and Tim Ross as a married couple having a frisky anniversary. But Ross has a secret… life, that is. He runs off to the office to rendezvous with Jyllyan Dixon, leaving Rachelle all alone.

Sort of.

Psycho-style shower scene aside, the film is less Hitchcock and more like an episode of the 1990s TV series *Silk Stalkings*, where hot women are knocked off, and equally smokin' ladies are there to be red herrings and occasionally the culprit.

Both Mark and Ryli play detectives investigating the initial murder, and Ryli looks especially born to the role, sporting a fashionable leather coat and a droll expression. Her real-life husband balances her with more intensity, while maintaining a certain detachment in keeping with his role.

If you pick up a David Lynch/*Twin Peaks* vibe from the proceedings, I suspect that was deliberate. Often in Lynch's morality plays, the detectives do little actual detecting. The thrill is in observing the parade of odd characters that people the landscape. That's doubly true of *Sin By Murder*, where one of the highlights is a flashback scene depicting Ryli and Jennifer Calhoun getting amorous.

I, for one, can't argue with that.

Jennifer and Ryli share a tender moment. Photo: Baranowski Archive.

MB: With my credit card debt still rising, it seemed Ryli and I wouldn't be moving back into a place of our own anytime soon. She even thought getting breast implants would be a good idea (which I'd be a fool to dispute), so there went another $1300. I was still only working part-time, but at least Ryli had her job at the Neurosurgery office, in the Medical Records department, to keep us afloat.

Meanwhile, I continued reaching out to potential distributors, as well as local media. I contacted Lawrence Toppman, film critic with *The Charlotte Observer*, who responded with keen interest in our work. He was especially impressed with the fact that we'd managed to get Brinke Stevens into our latest film. Ryli and I met him for an interview, and a

Teaser poster design #1. Photo: Baranowski Archive.

photographer named John Simmons later met us at home. John was hoping to get some shots of us working on a new project, but we had nothing in development. I hated to waste his time for a single publicity photo, so I quickly came up with an idea that nearly turned into our next feature—a killer clown film entitled *Beautiful Madness*.

Inspired by the titular song from Third Eye, a short-lived duo that included Australian musician Ollie Olsen, I decided that I would play the clown. I even purchased a complete outfit, including makeup and wig. As John photographed us, Ryli applied my makeup and we acted as if rehearsing a scene. A couple Sunday editions later, the photos showed up in the newspaper, enhancing Lawrence's already impressive article about us.

Teaser poster design #2. Photo: Baranowski Archive.

What should have been a celebratory moment, however, became one of dread, when Ryli suddenly began to worry what her bosses, co-workers and family would have to say about our "erotic horror" movies. From experience, she was especially concerned about losing her job, and at least while we were living with her parents, she wanted to create as little family drama as possible.

I fully understood, and perhaps I was slightly concerned about how my own bosses would respond. However, I would never apologize for my story ideas, nor for anything I'd asked Ryli to do—both as my wife, and as an actress. I never forced her into anything she wasn't comfortable doing, and as she herself put it, "if my interests and behavior surprises anybody, they never knew me." In the end, our fears were put to rest. No one had anything negative to say.

On the contrary, we were overwhelmed with supportive calls and emails from people in Charlotte, many who offered to help us in any way possible. One such person, Michael Hicks, would not only end up co-starring in my next film, but in nearly every one of my projects from that point on. Of course, there were others that merely wanted to use us to help bring their own artistic visions to life, or swinging couples who false-

Michael Hicks loses his cool. Photo: Baranowski Archive.

Tim and Jyllyan get cozy once more. Photo: Baranowski Archive.

ly assumed we did the same. It took us a few weeks to determine which relationships would be beneficial to all involved, and which ones were wastes of our time.

Speaking of time, it was around then that I heard back from David Sterling, a west coast producer and potential distributor to whom I'd recently sent screener copies of *Runaway Terror* and *Expendable*. He informed me that he greatly enjoyed both, and offered to distribute them as a double feature DVD. He even asked if I would be interested in directing a micro-budget erotic thriller for him, entitled *Blackmail*.

Although skeptical after our dealings with Everette and AEBN, I finally agreed. David's assistant sent me the script and a contract. Once signed, I received $400—just under half of the total budget for the film. I would get the rest upon completion, which had to be within two months.

My obsession had caused me to lose my mind.

Nevertheless, I read through the fifty-eight-page "script" and wondered how the hell I would turn it into an eighty-eight-minute movie, per the contract's requirement. It also called for no less than six love scenes, each with different partners. I informed David this simply wouldn't be

Ryli interrogates Stephen. Photo: Baranowski Archive.

possible... Not here, in the Bible Belt. Fortunately, David was willing to compromise.

The first thing I did was rewrote most of the existing screenplay, and then added an additional thirty pages to it. Somewhere along the way, I noticed that although the title was *Blackmail*, no actual blackmail took place in the story. I shrugged this off for the time being, finished with the script and then focused on casting.

Considering it was late 2003, at the height of the holiday season, and I had a month to shoot the entire film, I couldn't have asked for a better result. Rachelle was able to make the trip down from Ohio on short notice, Michael Hicks was anxious to play his first role, and Ryli was ready to show off her new and improved mammaries. I found a sporting actress from South Carolina, Jyllyan Dixon, who agreed to three love scenes, and a lead actor (Tim Ross) who was only there for the sexual thrill. Aside from his whispering, Clint Eastwood style of articulation, though, I had no complaints.

One actor, Stephen Elliott, traveled from Wilmington, North Carolina to play his part. He even provided us with our best interior location, a law office where his parents worked. There came an awkward moment where we ended up in an elevator with them, and they went on about how anxious they were to see the finished product. Considering we'd just used their office for a love scene (unbeknownst to them), I could only smile and nod.

Jennifer Calhoun was an actress who had just done a girl-girl photo shoot for an upcoming issue of *Hustler* magazine, and was playing Ryli's sexual partner in the film. She remarked how much she'd rather have worked with Ryli on the photo shoot than with Jenna Haze. Needless to say, her scenes with Ryli went well, even though Ryli's grandfather had just passed away that morning, making for an otherwise difficult day of shooting for her. I felt badly for not packing it in and rescheduling the day's scenes, but Jennifer had driven hours to be there, and we were using a location that wouldn't be available again.

Finally, I offered a small role to a close friend named Lauren Brower, who fronted a local band that also included her husband, Scott, who played drums. She and I had met through David, the interviewer for *Reel Carolina*, who recommended me as a photographer to take some intimate pictures of her as a surprise birthday present for Scott. Sadly, she was suffering from cancer, and already had some tissue removed from her breast. The pictures weren't just for Scott, she told me, but for herself. She needed reassuring that she was still attractive. I was more than happy to oblige, and I was honored to have her accept the role as a detective in the film... just as I was heartbroken when she passed away, a few years later.

Jennifer and Ryli. Photo: Baranowski Archive.

Lauren. (R.I.P.) Photo: Baranowski Archive.

Although I shot the interior scenes in Charlotte, exteriors were shot in St. Augustine, Florida, during a trip there to visit my mother for the holidays. It's one of my favorite places to visit, and one of the things I like most about the film.

Because I didn't have time to create enough music for the entire film, I contacted the aforementioned Ollie Olsen, hoping he would allow me to incorporate a few songs from one of his solo albums into the soundtrack. I was shocked by his incredible generosity when he permitted me to do so at no cost. These compositions are another of the film's high points, in my opinion. Also featured is False Profits Coalition, a hip-hop act representing Buffalo, New York.

With the film shot, scored and edited to my own liking, I sent a screener disc to David for his review. Until finally hearing back from him a few days later, I dreaded that he wouldn't be happy with it, or that he'd demand re-shoots. Instead, he loved it just as it was, and sent me the remainder of the $1000 budget. At the request of the Executive Producer, the title was then changed to *Sin by Murder*. I didn't care much for that,

Mark shooting exteriors in St. Augustine, FL. Photo: Baranowski Archive.

but at least it made more sense than calling the film *Blackmail* when it didn't involve any.

Interestingly enough, I discovered what that was all about when David sent me another script for a follow-up to *Sin*. That second script actually belonged to the *Blackmail* cover page sent with the *Sin* script, and vice versa. Turns out *Sin* was originally called *The Big Lie*....

Anyway, after agreeing to take on *Sin*, I told David that would be my last erotic thriller. He either misunderstood or was so impressed with my work on *Sin* that he ignored me, because the true *Blackmail* script was identical to the first draft of *Sin*, only more mundane. In any case, he wanted me to direct six more films for him that year, each with the same $1000 budget! I may have been obsessed, but I hadn't lost my common sense; I strongly declined.

For that reason, perhaps, the *Runaway Terror / Expendable* double feature DVD never materialized. Still, David claimed ownership of both titles when another distributor later approached me with a distribution

DVD box cover art (Second edition). Photo: Baranowski Archive.

offer for *Expendable*, but I'd never signed any contract with David relating to either film. The second offer went away, and I haven't heard a word from David since.

Another lesson learned.

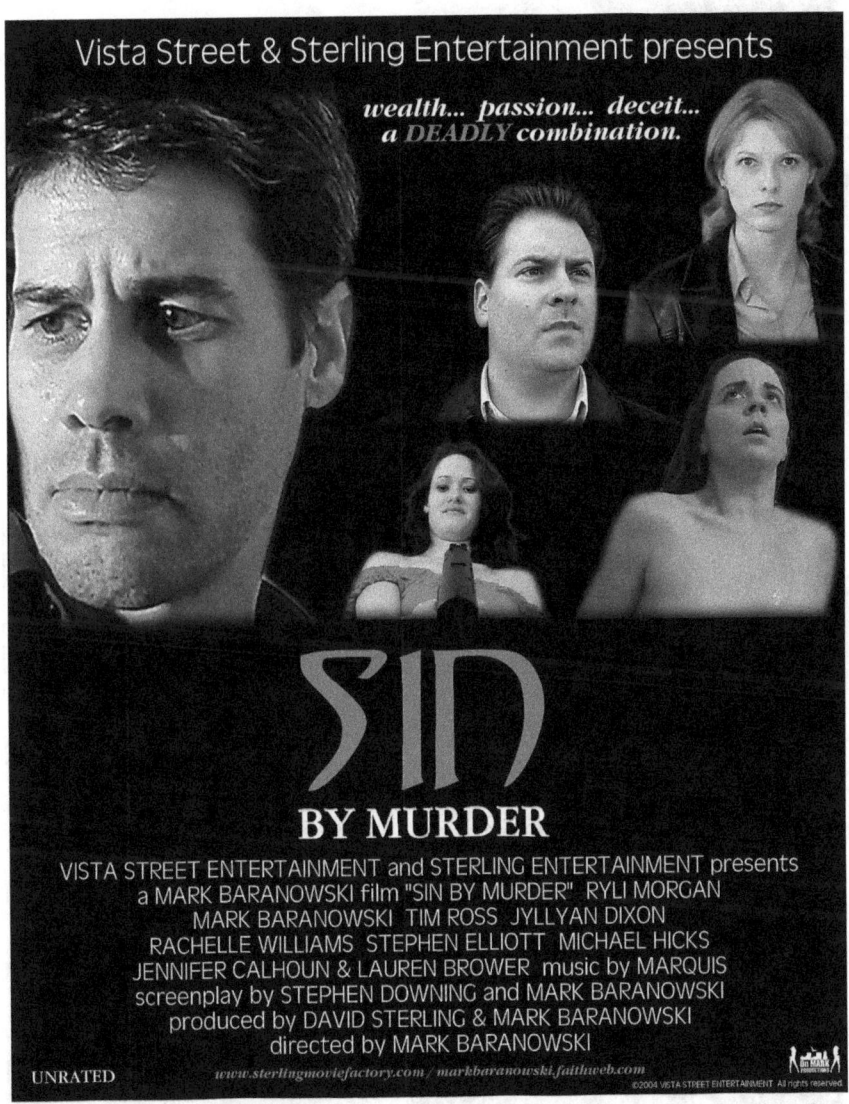

Poster design. Photo: Baranowski Archive.

Alternate poster design. Photo: Baranowski Archive.

Ad design for *Rue Morgue* magazine. Photo: Baranowski Archive.

DVD box cover art. Photo: Baranowski Archive.

6

The Powerful Play

Release date: August 13, 2004
Director: Mark Baranowski
Writer: Mark Baranowski
Producer: Mark Baranowski
Music: MARQUIS (Mark Baranowski)
Genre: Music
Runtime: 88 minutes
Cast: Mark Baranowski, Ryli Morgan, Tracy Ellis, James McGriff, Jennifer Cafarelli, Michael Hicks, Rachelle Williams, Patricia White, Brinke Stevens, Joshua Thrailkill
Plot: *The Powerful Play* begins with a collection of seven music videos that accompany the jazzy-funky instrumentals off Mark's 2002 album, *The Flesh & Blood Show* (performed under his MARQUIS pseudonym). The videos feature an assortment of his closest friends and family, and present Mark's own visions of love, life, lust, death, and the afterlife. "Living and Re-living The Powerful Play" is a short film that includes an in-depth interview with Mark himself, along with home video segments and behind-the-scenes footage.

SKB: Less a feature film than a collection of music videos, these seven mini-movies are glimpses into Mark's favorite subjects. They also utilize pieces from some of his early films, as well as point toward areas he would explore in the future.

If you haven't watched this collection, it's worth looking for; it illustrates how, as a filmmaker, you can use the medium of music videos to work out various concepts. You never know when you might want to expand such a piece into a feature later on, and it's good to have a starting point.

Mark and Ryli have the most—and biggest—roles in the proceedings, but Tracy Ellis, Michael Hicks, Rachelle Williams, and Patricia White all play key parts.

As you might expect, most of these shorts are wordless, with just Mark's instrumental tracks helping to pull together the images. The vi-

Stare-down on the stairs: Patricia, Ryli, and Rachelle. Photo: Baranowski Archive.

An introspective Mark. Photo: Baranowski Archive.

suals themselves are rendered in black-and-white, which makes them feel even more like you dug through your parents' closet and unearthed something they shot forty years ago.

The stories are non-narrative, allowing the viewer to ruminate on Mark's explorations of love, death, family life, and the creative process. The pieces range from funny, to sad, to creepy, with a continual overlap (you never know, in one of Mark's films, when a mundane or tender moment will turn deadly).

A reprise video shows elements of all of his concepts, and serves as a reminder of the things in our lives that comfort—or torment—us.

MB: Ever since the late 1980's, I've been a musician of various sorts, starting with rap and moving on to light R&B, electronic, and then back to rap. On average, I made at least one album per year from 1997 to 2010. *The Powerful Play* brought attention to my musical side, with a specific focus on my 2002 instrumental album, *The Flesh & Blood Show*. A Pete Walker horror film inspired the album's title, while both titles were metaphors for life itself. Such was the beginning of my more personal, soul-searching period of filmmaking....

This experimental project consisted of a black-and-white music video for each song on the album, followed by a lengthy interview with yours truly that brings viewers up to date with my art, music, and film work. It's all done rather tongue-in-cheek, and the music videos were especially enjoyable to shoot.

The first, "Can I Have a Kiss," again took place at Ryli's parents' house, and introduced our Dachshund puppy, Nixie. I threw in some silent film-style dialogue with a nod to one of my favorite films, *Alien Predator* (1985), just to have Ryli punch me in the mouth. Nixie, who'd just secretly licked her nether regions, would then kiss it all better. Fun stuff!

"Born to Die" was a much more somber affair. While Ryli mourns a lost loved one, we meet that person's spirit, played by Tracy Ellis, a local model-actress that I'd hoped to continue working with beyond *The Powerful Play*. She makes her way through the cemetery, initially unaware of her new state of being, and then unwilling to accept it. I play another spirit, who welcomes her and helps her find peace. For this video, I in-

Mark and Nixie in "Can I Have a Kiss?". Photo: Baranowski Archive.

Mark and Tracy in "Born to Die". Photo: Baranowski Archive.

cluded a scene from another of my favorite Italian films, *Dellamorte Dellamore* (1994).

For "Victims," we were finally able to work with our friend, Jennifer, from Cuyahoga Falls, Ohio. I shot this during a convention at the circular Quaker Square hotel in Akron, where she came to visit Ryli and I for the weekend. Her character was the client of a high-priced escort, played by Ryli. While in bed, Ryli is plagued with visions of a malevolent clown (myself, in the footage we'd shot for *The Charlotte Observer* article) that cause her to lure her client into the bathtub, where she kills her.

"Money" was a light-hearted romp that involved my now-good buddy, Michael Hicks, and myself as we drove through Charlotte, anxious to get back home to our sweethearts, played by Tracy and Ryli. Although the title had nothing to do with the events in the video, the original song contained a relevant and poignant sample that I love, from the film *Swingers* (1996).

"The Pain Helps" gave our long-time fans what they wanted, or at least what they expected. I play myself, basically—the exploitation director who's tormented by the seductive visions he's captured on film. He tries desperately, in vain, to shake (or stroke, as my movements suggest)

Ryli and Jennifer in "Victims". Photo: Baranowski Archive.

Michael likes what he sees: "Money". Photo: Baranowski Archive.

Tracy exposed: "The Pain Helps". Photo: Baranowski Archive.

away the memories of beautiful, naked women while his spiritual side attempts to take over.

I shot "Live to Create" while at my day job, to examine the tasks and creations of different species; birds and insects, along with my actual coworkers and myself. Later in the video, I inserted shots of various local churches, as if the work we were doing was for the sake of a greater good. That message gets a bit clouded at the end, however, as I wearily punch my time card, don my shades and stroll out of the building to do the things that matter more to me.

Finally, "The Powerful Play" is a collection of outtakes from each of the previous videos, meant to celebrate everyone involved not only in this project, but also in my life. It was my way of reflecting on them, and reveling in the good times and laughter we all shared during production. If *The Powerful Play* had a message, it was summed up in this video.... Enjoy what you do, treasure your life and the people in it—and smile often.

For the DVD, I conducted cast interviews, created a rough cut of *The Zombie Room*, and compiled the many bloopers from that shoot for the end credits of *The Powerful Play* itself. Also included was home video

Creatures great and small: "Live to Create". Photo: Baranowski Archive.

Speaking in tongues: "The Powerful Play". Photo: Baranowski Archive.

Mark: "Keep smilin'!" Photo: Baranowski Archive.

footage revealing a much younger me, as I shared some memorable moments with family and friends.

Admittedly, *The Powerful Play* was a hard sell. Neither a proper documentary nor music film, it appealed mainly to those already familiar with my work. That was fine with me then, and still is.... From the feedback I've received from those who've seen it, it's a winner, nonetheless. As this and my forthcoming films would reveal, the beauty of being truly independent is that there are no rules to follow, no reason to limit oneself to a specific audience. The alternative just might have allowed me to finally turn my hobby into my job, but after having complete creative control for so long, I saw no alternative at all.

DVD box cover art (First edition). Photo: Baranowski Archive.

7

Heaven Help Me I'm in Love

Release date: September 27, 2005
Director: Mark Baranowski
Writer: Mark Baranowski (with additional material by Ryli Morgan)
Producer: Mark Baranowski
Music: MARQUIS (Mark Baranowski), Awful Goodness (Mark Baranowski & Ryli Morgan)
Genre: Comedy, Drama, Romance
Runtime: 98 minutes
Cast: Mark Baranowski, Ryli Morgan, Michael Hicks, Minna Hicks, Rachelle Williams, Lynn Lowry, Brinke Stevens, Tom McCaffery, Nic Pesante, Heather Toon, England Simpson, Todd Brown, Jimmy Moore, Conney Lemke, B. Dallas Jones.
Plot: Butch and Angie are in love, but their relationship isn't progressing quickly enough for Angie. When Butch foolishly attempts to deceive her on account of a friend, whom she already dislikes, she decides to call it quits, and dumps him. Meanwhile, screenwriter Donald—another of Butch's friends—is having his own problems in dealing with writer's block and a wife who's tired of being ignored. Struggling desperately to write the All-American comedy, Donald soon finds inspiration in Butch.... A devious ex-girlfriend, a pushy drug dealer, a blind date gone awry, and a nagging mother turns Butch's weekend—and spirits—from bad to downright pathetic. As Angie tends to her ailing mother and begins to accept life without him, Butch races to make amends, in an effort to win back her heart before it's too late.

Mark and Ryli get intimate. Photo: Baranowski Archive.

SKB: Another spoiler alert: no one dies in this Baranowski production. That may seem completely out of character to many of the couple's admirers. It's Babe Ruth without a bat, Jeff Beck sans guitar, and Lady Gaga in an off-the-rack T-shirt and jeans.

Michael and Minna Hicks. Photo: Baranowski Archive.

If looks could kill: Ryli and Rachelle. Photo: Baranowski Archive.

But any fans that have been paying attention couldn't help but notice from the start the strong romantic streak in Mark's work. Not "romantic" in the sense of Hallmark cards with two swans swimming into the sunset; more like… the world is supposed to operate in a certain way; with justice, fair play, and love. Even at his most cynical, there is a sense in Mark's scripts that there is right and wrong, and consequences for choices.

So, a rom-com is not really out of left field for him, and this one absolutely isn't.

You'll not only see a lot of familiar faces from his stable of actors (Ryli, Rachelle Williams, Michael Hicks, et al.), you'll also notice one of his favorite themes: how unbearably awkward relationships are. In this movie, the way that the characters relate to each other is clumsier than a newborn baby giraffe. Jerry Seinfeld's dysfunctional friends have nothing on this group.

This leads to a lot of laughs, as when Mark tries to pass off a friend that his girlfriend dislikes as someone else entirely, or when Rachelle shows up to basically ravage Mark (you'll note, he offers very little resistance… and neither would any of us), and then Ryli walks in. Oops.

Throughout, the film plays like a loose Cassavetes riff on male bonding, female friendships, the strains of marriage, and how hard it is to actu-

Photo: Baranowski Archive.

Brinke Stevens. Photo: Baranowski Archive.

ally grow up. A Shakespearean side note shows us Hicks as a screenwriter seeking inspiration, support, and the attention of Hollywood. Mark's own experiences are clearly reflected in this subplot.

There is a serious side, too, with Brinke Stevens portraying Ryli's mom, who shows concern for her daughter's fractured relationship, all the while battling a brain tumor.

This may be one of Mark's few movies with a happy ending, which should tell us all something about his true views.

MB: This film marked the turning point for Ryli and I, in a number of ways. I needed to distance myself from the "Porn King" stigma I carried, especial-

DVD box cover art (Second edition). Photo: Baranowski Archive.

Mark and Ryli: Trouble in paradise. Photo: Baranowski Archive.

ly within the Bible Belt. Meanwhile, Ryli tired of being "the naked chick," and wanted a role with more depth than any she'd ever played before.

On a personal level, there was tension steadily building in our relationship. We'd been married for over four years, with not one mention of

A further troubled Ryli. Photo: Baranowski Archive.

ever having children. I was working full-time again, but I was no less obsessed with making one film (or album) after another. I'd neglected Teresa in favor of Ryli for too long.

At the same time, we'd worn out our welcome at her parents' house. We weren't earning our keep, and *Expendable* had come back to haunt us. Someone who'd ordered a copy by mail and paid with a check turned out to be a 14-year-old boy. The name on the check was his mother's, and "her" signature turned out to be a forgery. She reported us to the Postmaster General for selling pornographic materials to a minor. The day the mailman came to the door to inform Ryli's mother of this was a harrowing one, indeed.

In record time, we moved into an apartment only slightly larger than our last. It was located five minutes away from Ryli's parents' house, which made moving convenient, at least. Although Ryli was sure we'd end up in jail for the *Expendable* situation, nothing more ever came of it.

Once we were settled into our new surroundings, I started work on a script that revolved around relationship issues that Ryli and I were dealing with, as well as some I'd experienced with old girlfriends. In the process, I also created a character much like myself, who was striving for his

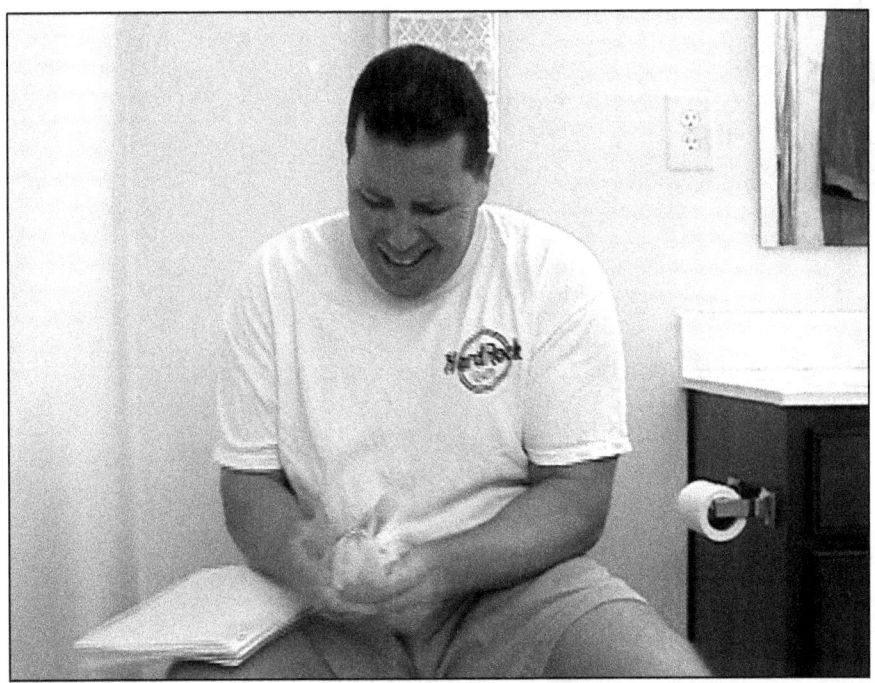

Michael Hicks as the frustrated filmmaker. Photo: Baranowski Archive.

big break in movies. This allowed me to vent, in a roundabout way (since it wasn't my character doing the venting), about certain things and people I viewed unfavorably as such.

In doing so, however, I alienated myself from several of our peers, with whom we'd attended conventions, collaborated and supported for three years prior. In their minds, I wasn't being a "team player," and had unfairly criticized someone (actress Debbie Rochon, for the curious) they'd befriended long before meeting Ryli and I.

Loyalty. I respect that. Now, since I was never given the chance to explain myself, let's examine the trouble-making dialogue, word for word:

> BUTCH
> How'd you shoot this?

CU of Donald. He becomes increasingly irritated from this point on.

> DONALD
> With a video camera!

CU of Butch.

> BUTCH
> What model?

CU of Donald.

> DONALD
> What's the fucking difference?

CU of Butch. After a beat, he slowly looks over at Donald.

> BUTCH
> What's your problem?

CU of Donald. He's quite upset.

> DONALD
> My <u>problem</u> is having to reveal to the world
> what fucking equipment I use to make <u>my</u>

movies! It wouldn't bother me if people
weren't so damn judgmental about it!

ECU of Donald.

> DONALD (CONT'D)
> Don, you need better lighting! Don, you need
> more lenses! Don, you need to get a better
> camera, preferably one with a mic input!
> Don, you should really be shooting on film
> instead of video!

LOW DUTCH ANGLE CU of Donald.

> DONALD (CONT'D)
> Hey people, just watch the movie and
> shut the fuck up!

CU of both. Butch stares at Donald as he continues ranting, still glaring at the TV screen.

> DONALD (CONT'D)
> Everybody's a jaded fucking critic, nowadays!
> After havin' their senses raped by one Star Wars
> or Lord of the Rings movie after another, who
> wants to look at some shitty little independent
> movies like mine?

HIGH ANGLE CU of Donald.

> DONALD (CONT'D)
> Do I need to be like all the other no-budget
> directors, too, and cast Debbie Rochon just to
> get my movies noticed? Well, I'm sorry....

ECU of Donald's mouth.

> DONALD (CONT'D)
> ... but I happen to not <u>like</u> Debbie Rochon!

ECU of Donald.

> DONALD (CONT'D)
> So if that means that my work is destined to remain either unwatched or criticized....

CU of both.

> DONALD (CONT'D)
> ... so fuckin' be it.

Mark and his trusty PV-DV52D. Photo: Baranowski Archive.

Every B-to-Z-grade filmmaker I met put Butch's first few questions to me. Donald's defensive responses are what went through my head, each time. As if we were all supposed to be using the same camera model, I was given either a blank stare or a chuckle of derision upon divulging my choice tool of the trade. For those I never bothered to answer, let it be known that I relied on a single camera from 2003 to 2011: a Panasonic PV-DV52D. Light, compact, and simple. Look it up.

To this day, Ryli tells me it might have been to our benefit if I hadn't been so quick to dismiss the helpful advice of our peers. Perhaps. Perhaps not. I'll admit, I'm as stubborn as they come, but if I wanted to do the same as everyone else, I'd have gone to film school.

As for Debbie… I wrote the script for *Heaven Help Me, I'm in Love* shortly after watching *Something to Scream About* (2003), a documentary about B-Movie actresses. Throughout her segments of the film, Debbie came across to me as unhappy and resentful, believing she's above the material that she's best known and adored for. She mentions how little money she makes from these films, even warns potential "Scream Queens" against them, yet she's still the one everyone wants to work with. Therefore, my criticism during Donald's rant was less directed at Debbie than it was at the smitten fan boys with cameras who seem to think that casting her is all it takes to make a hit feature for the home video market.

I should mention that I met Debbie before watching the documentary. Ryli and I were guests, as was she, at the Frightvision convention in Cleveland, Ohio, a year earlier. We'd ventured out from behind our

Mark looks on as Donald spouts off. Photo: Baranowski Archive.

98 • *From Despair to Beloved*

Michael and Minna. Photo: Baranowski Archive.

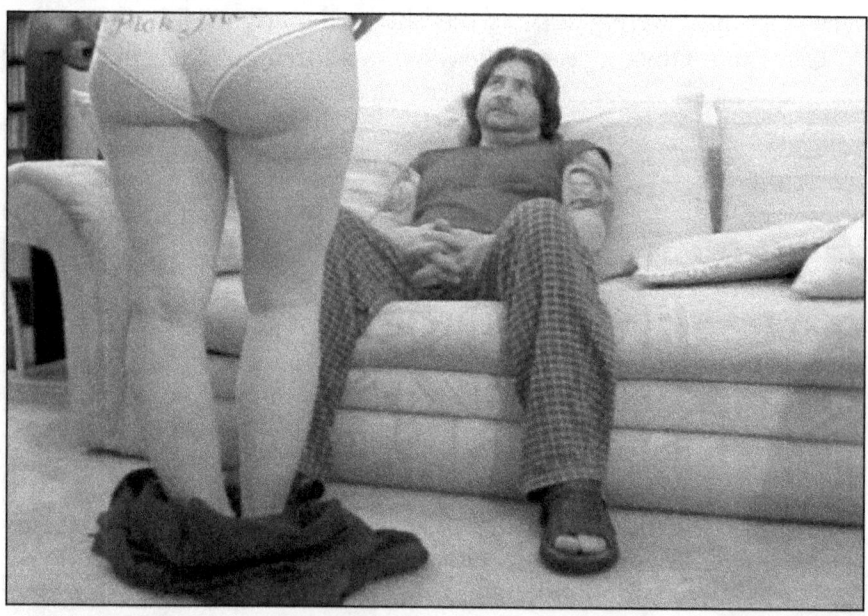
Rachelle makes things hard for Mark. Photo: Baranowski Archive.

table and made our way to hers, only to be let down by her uncaring and disinterested response to our introduction. From there, in full view of her table, we chatted with one of Ryli's buddies, special effects artist and actor Tom Savini, whom Debbie had just spoken to with excitement. By the looks of things, she reserved her energy for famous folks such as Tom, and the aforementioned fan boys. No big deal, really, since many convention guests act this way... but you have to admit, the "I happen to not like Debbie Rochon" line was warranted.

Doesn't matter. Moving on....

Plain and simple, *Heaven* was a sheer joy to make. For the roles of the frustrated writer-director and his impatient wife, I chose Michael Hicks and his (then) real-life wife, Minna, who did quite well for her first acting gig. I was more interested in the couple's natural dynamic than the fact that she was new to all this. They didn't disappoint.

Rachelle returned to our bathtub once again, making the Canton-to-Charlotte road trip early in the day, completing her scenes and then returning home, that evening. To show our appreciation to her driver, we put the two of them together for an amusing scene at the end of the film. The highlight of her visit, of course, happened when she climbed, naked, into my lap and tried her hardest to get me aroused as Ryli shot the scene... Yes, this life's been very, very good to me.

Nic Pesante as the no-nonsense "Guy". Photo: Baranowski Archive.

One of our peers from the convention circuit, Nic Pesante, drove down from Pennsylvania to play "Guy," the drug dealer. He discovered upon arriving that we had no choice but to start shooting his scenes immediately, due to Michael Hicks' limited schedule. Stressful, but all worked out as it was supposed to. Nic spent the night at our apartment, went out for breakfast with us the next morning, and then headed home, sooner than expected.

Local actress England Simpson and not-so-local actor Tom McCaffery, who drove to Charlotte from Wilmington at the last minute, played two fan-favorite characters. I hadn't yet met Tom—or seen him, for that matter—before he arrived, but in talking to him the day before, I felt confident in his abilities to pull off the character of "Stu," a pot-smoking slacker. Fortunately, he did so with flying colors. England did a terrific job as the girl-next-door-turned-dominatrix, and I still applaud her for embracing such a character and making it her own.

A few more local actors and friends rounded out the supporting cast, such as Todd Brown (lead singer for Withstand, a local hard rock band), who also provided us with a last-minute location when we needed one, and Jimmy Moore, a good ol' boy who worked in the maintenance department for one of the local school systems. He'd always wanted to try

Mark and Tom, trying not to laugh. Photo: Baranowski Archive.

Good-girl-turned-bad, England Simpson. Photo: Baranowski Archive.

his hand at acting, and I was happy to give him a shot. He nailed it.

I mention the film's "celebrities" last, because they were the last to perform. From the start, I wanted well-known ladies to play the mothers of Ryli's character and my own. However, I wasn't sure yet who would be

Todd Brown. Photo: Baranowski Archive.

Jimmy Moore teaches Mark a thing or two. Photo: Baranowski Archive.

most suitable, who would be available, or whom I could afford. Brinke worked out best for the part of Ryli's mother, which thrilled me because I'd wanted to work with her in the flesh since *Expendable*, two years earlier. Still clueless as to who would play mine, I suddenly recalled a recent

Behind the scenes with Ryli, Brinke, and Mark. Photo: Baranowski Archive.

short film I'd seen about actress Lynn Lowry. I thought she was terrific, so I located her online and emailed her. She responded with great interest in the project, stating she wanted a part that she could "… sink her teeth into." After reading the script and eventually realizing it wasn't another horror film, she graciously accepted.

Both Brinke and Lynn were content to stay in our small apartment with us during their respective weekend visits. When we weren't working, we took them out to dinner, or picked up anything they asked for from the grocery store. With Brinke, there was even time to go see a movie (*The Devil's Rejects*, which she felt slighted for not having been asked to play a part in, considering its cast of long-time genre greats). Aside from one awkward moment with Lynn, when I got a bit too excited about the Bee Gees, we all had a blast. Working together couldn't have gone smoother, and our leisure time couldn't have been more fun. It was terribly sad to see them go.

To Brinke and Lynn, this project may have just been another paycheck. To me, however, it was a monumental event, not to mention a refreshing change to see both of these horror film veterans playing something other than psychopaths or victims in peril. Their fans might not share my opinion, but if these two great talents were willing to step outside of their comfort zone, why not?

Ryli, Lynn, and Mark. Photo: Baranowski Archive.

When production wrapped, I expected to jump right into the editing process, as usual. However, Ryli had been experiencing a racing heartbeat (she'd been diagnosed with Wolff-Parkinson-White syndrome as a child), and went to her doctor in concern. Upon examination, it was determined that immediate corrective surgery would be required—for the second time in her life.

It was only when the ordeal was over, and Ryli was in the clear, that I took calls from concerned friends and family. One of those calls came from the peers I'd later offend with my "Debbie" dialogue. After giving

Mark, below the Visulite marquee. Photo: Baranowski Archive.

Scott and Lauren Brower with Mark and Ryli. Photo: Baranowski Archive.

them an update on Ryli's condition, I commented on how fortunate it was that we'd finished shooting the film before this happened. Whether that was my obsession talking or I'd truly become that selfish, the comment went over like a lead balloon. From that point on, my relationship with them continually went downhill.

Once Ryli had fully recovered, I was able to finish post-production on *Heaven*. I was so pleased with the end result that I felt it deserved a proper local premiere. I contacted the management of Charlotte's Visulite Theater (the city's oldest art house theater, now better known as a live music venue), and scheduled the premiere to take place there the following week. Once again, Lawrence Toppman covered the film and announced the premiere in *The Charlotte Observer*. He'd also interviewed Brinke while she was in town, and her Sunday feature ran alongside ours.

For a rainy Friday night, we couldn't have hoped for a better turnout. Both Ryli's and my own co-workers showed up, along with Lauren and Scott Brower. Cast members were there, as were old friends, independent film supporters, and casual weekend moviegoers. Pictures were taken afterward, and even autographs were signed. It was truly a night to remember.

Sadly, the joy of the event was to be short-lived. Ryli and I had been invited to another convention in Wisconsin that was to take place in a few short weeks. In the meantime, however, the tension between us had reached a breaking point. We separated, and she moved back into her parents' house. I canceled our appearance with the convention promoter, and then sank into a well-deserved depression. After all, our marital problems were caused by my stubbornness, my selfishness, and my obsession.

For weeks, I left the apartment only when it was time to play locksmith.

Photo: Baranowski Archive.

Heaven Help Me I'm In Love

Promotional flyer for the *Heaven* premiere. Photo: Baranowski Archive.

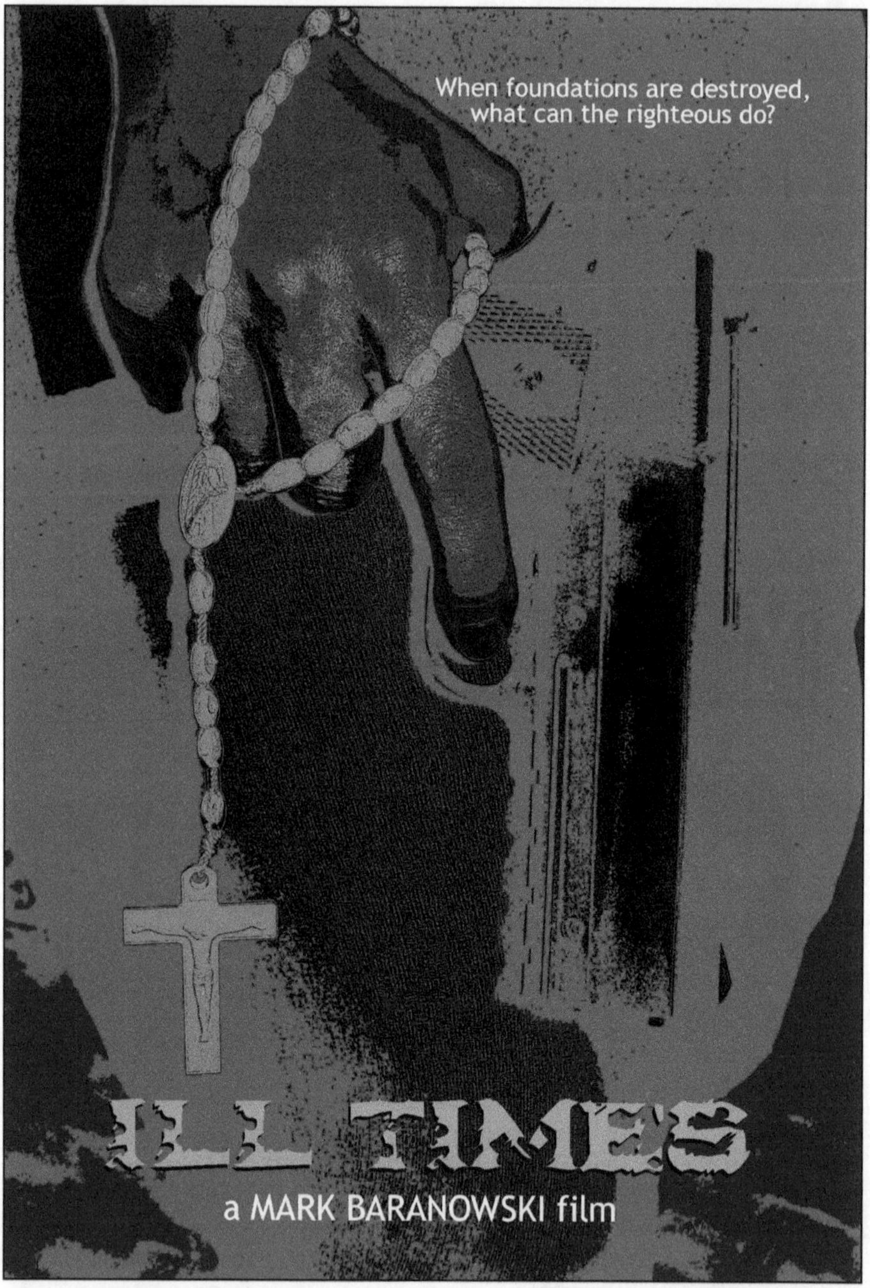

Poster and DVD box cover art. Photo: Baranowski Archive.

8

Ill Times

Release date: May 5, 2009
Director: Mark Baranowski
Writer: Mark Baranowski
Producer: Mark Baranowski
Music: MARQUIS/The Marksman (both Mark Baranowski), Awful Goodness (Mark Baranowski & Ryli Morgan), Mister Blue, Withstand, Mego
Genre: Crime, Drama
Runtime: 69 minutes
Cast: Mister Blue, Ernest Broome, Todd Brown, Dennis Cothran, Michael Hicks, Hayley Lakeman, Travis Lakeman, Conney Lemke, James McGriff, Mimi, Ryli Morgan (as Teresa Baranowski), Eryk Baranowski, Felicia Poirier, Demond Reed, England Simpson, Paris Simpson.
Plot: A day (the last, for some) in the lives of a care-free sex fiend; a promiscuous small-time gangster; a desperate single mother; a grieving widow; a vengeful female drug-dealer; a wretched heroin addict; an abused wife; a conniving husband; a shady hit man; an innocent rape victim; a lonely and dangerous stalker; and a guilt-ridden father. Their stories intersect to create this gritty urban drama.

SKB: Together with his next film, *Mister Dissolute*, this is Mark at his most "urban." *Ill Times* wouldn't look out of place in a film festival playing alongside *Boyz n the Hood* (1991), and perhaps that's what Mark was striving for—the idea that the "hood" is wherever you are, and the toll of a life lived for drug use is unchanging.

A victim's last sight. Photo: Baranowski Archive.

Truthfully, you would need an abacus to add up all the lives ruined by the end of the movie. It's not coincidental that the passions that unfold over the sixty-nine-minute running time are Biblical in scope. Trust, betrayal, love, and jealousy combine and collide as the desires of some are thwarted so that others can get what they want.

The wretched addict: Mimi. Photo: Baranowski Archive.

The themes explored in *Ill Times* complement a movie such as Darren Aronofsky's *Requiem for a Dream* (2000), which was based on a book by Hubert Selby, Jr. Selby also wrote the iconic novel *Last Exit to Brooklyn*, which drove the Old Testament and inner city life at each other like freight trains with the throttles stuck. You expect to see choices go horribly wrong in such a film, and they assuredly do here, as when a drug addict winds up being raped while she is passed out.

Fittingly, there are many dream-like elements, including the fact that most of the action seems to be taking place in the same house (seen in different rooms from various angles), and the story zigzags from episode to episode, without a direct through-line.

Telling, too, is that the only point of calm in the narrative is Ryli, billed under her actual name, in a scene where she is in real-life mom-mode, playing with her son.

MB: By some miracle, Ryli and I reconciled in early 2006. Many changes needed to be made, however, since much would happen to us during the next three years. Ryli became pregnant with our first child, and then decided she'd had enough of being "Ryli Morgan." Before going back to a life where she was only Teresa, however, she was the cover model for *Draculina* magazine's fifty-first issue, where she announced her retirement from acting. Shortly after, we released *The Ryli Morgan Collection*, a

Teresa and Eryk. Photo: Baranowski Archive.

DVD for which I re-edited our first four films, and included several "Ryli-approved" bonus features. It soon became our best-selling title.

In 2008, we finally bought a house of our own, and with the $7500 First-time Homebuyer tax credit, we were able to get started on a new film in 2009 that was unlike any we'd made before. Even Ryli would be a small part of it, although choosing to be credited by her legal name. Called *Ill Times* (the same title of a song from my 2006 rap album, *The Reason I*

Ryli Morgan: Cover Girl! Photo courtesy Rick Rorie/Draculina Publishing.

DVD box cover art. Photo courtesy Rick Rorie/Baranowski Archive.

The foxy Felicia Poirier. Photo: Baranowski Archive.

Hayley Lakeman fears the worst. Photo: Baranowski Archive.

Put This Together), it was an urban drama I'd recently written that would showcase my rap music, as well as that of a new co-worker and a FedEx driver that delivered to my day job. It would feature an ensemble cast, all revolving around one location that was meant to represent several. Confusing, perhaps, but the point was that if the audience is engrossed in the story, the characters' surroundings are irrelevant.

Many consider this my best film, whether due to its realism, the characters, or lack of nudity (finally, praise from the Bible belt!). Perhaps my not being in it was a benefit, since it allowed me to shoot the film myself, from start to finish. Having one less task on my plate was certainly a welcome change, in any case.

In casting *Ill Times*, I'd come full circle, relying on several enthusiastic friends and co-workers with little or no acting experience. This included Mister Blue, the FedEx driver/rapper; Hayley Lakeman, my tattoo artist; Demond Reed, another rapper; and Paris Simpson, England's sister. Eng-

The menacing Todd Brown. Photo: Baranowski Archive.

land, herself, returned to play a major role, along with Todd Brown, Michael Hicks, Conney Lemke (who'd briefly appeared in *Heaven Help Me, I'm in Love*), and James McGriff (first seen in *The Powerful Play*). Even my son, Eryk, played a small part and proved he's a natural-born actor.

As a special surprise to Ryli, I dedicated the film to her mother, who'd passed away earlier that year.

Sisters England and Paris Simpson. Photo: Baranowski Archive.

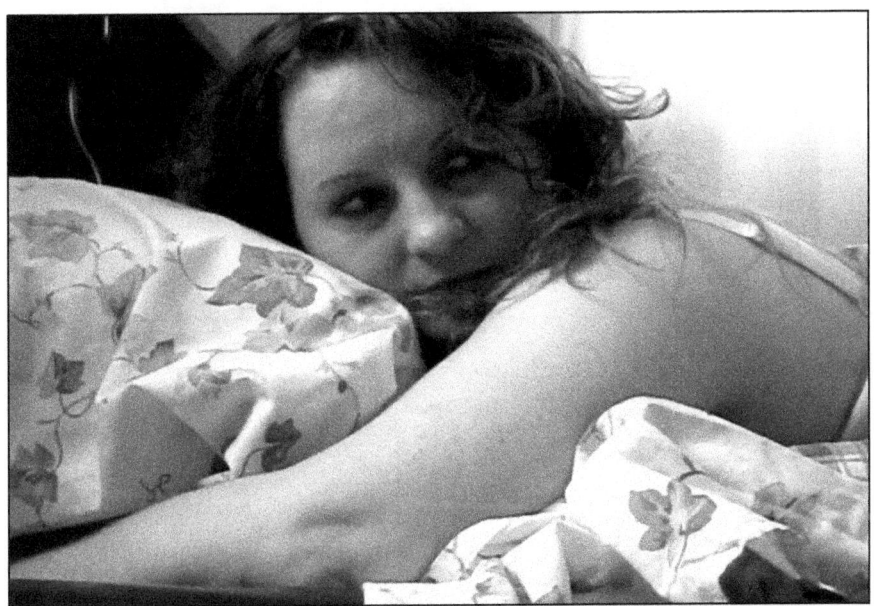

Used and discarded: Conney Lemke. Photo: Baranowski Archive.

Ernest Broome retaliates. Photo: Baranowski Archive.

Travis Lakeman as the betrayed husband. Photo: Baranowski Archive.

Ill Times • 119

Mister Blue practices intimidation by phone. Photo: Baranowski Archive.

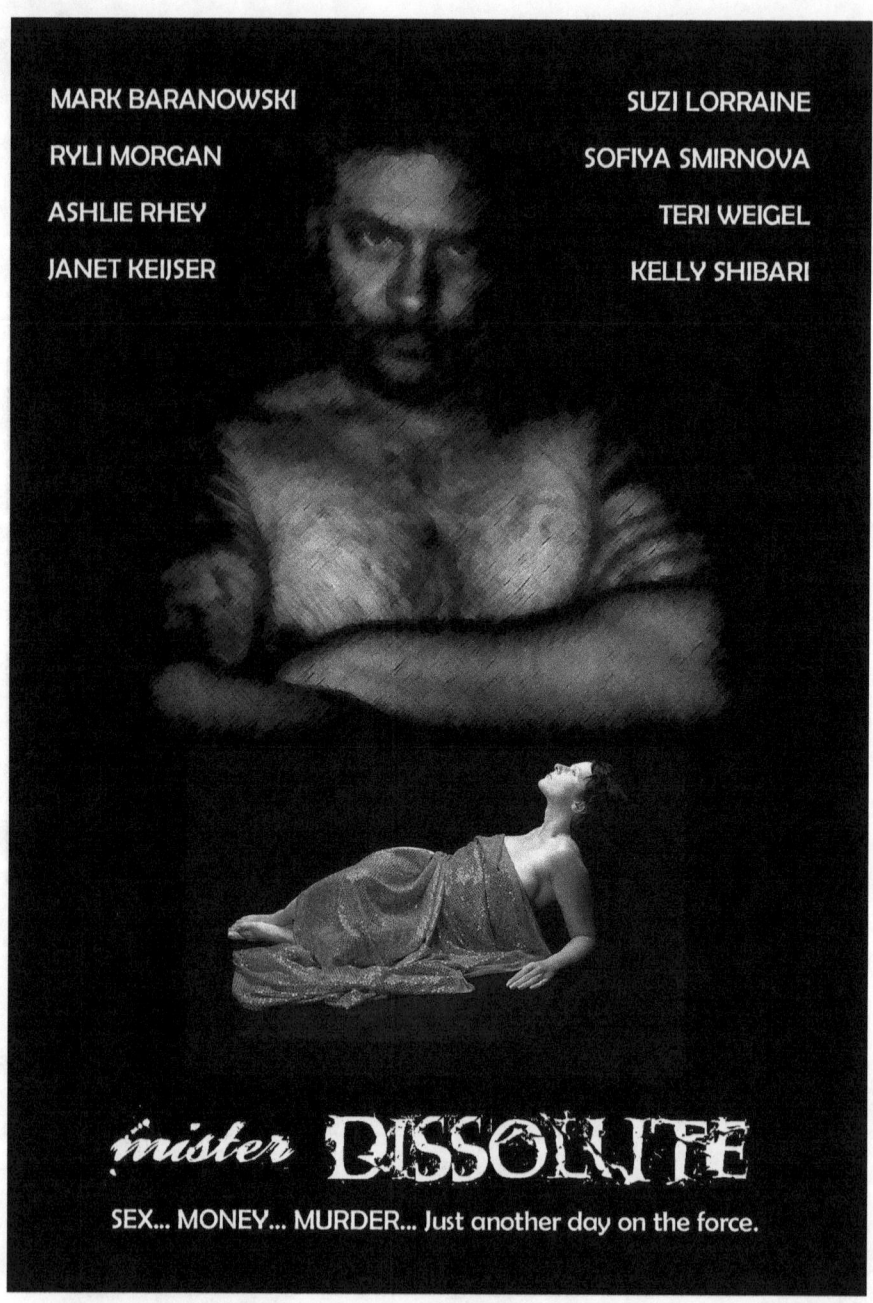

DVD box cover art. Photo: Baranowski Archive.

10

Mister Dissolute

Release date: November 24, 2009
Director: Mark Baranowski
Writer: Mark Baranowski
Producer: Mark Baranowski
Music: MARQUIS (Mark Baranowski), Brick by Brick Productions (Demond Reed)
Genre: Crime, Drama, Thriller
Runtime: 78 minutes
Cast: Mark Baranowski, Ashlie Rhey, Ryli Morgan, Janet Keijser, Sofiya Smirnova, Anna Engels, Demond Reed, Teri Weigel, Maria Kil, Kelly Shibari, Suzi Lorraine, Patrick G. Keenan, Mister Blue, Phillip Smith, Josh Lute, Ellen Rodillo-Fowler, Joseph Bey
Plot: Meet corrupt detectives Ron Fugate and Morris Brinson—the former obsessed by sex and drugs, the latter motivated solely by money. When a criminal they put behind bars is released from prison and puts a hit out on them, both their partnership and their very existence quickly begins to decay.... Who will survive, and at what cost?

SKB: Mark's movies have always existed in a strange twilight between urban and suburban. The landscape is distinctly suburbs, with images of lemonade and lawnmowers, but the action could be taking place in a grimy downtown club.

Nowhere is this truer than in *Mister Dissolute,* a riff on the "Bad Detective" genre, where the lead character is a cop with a drug/sex/

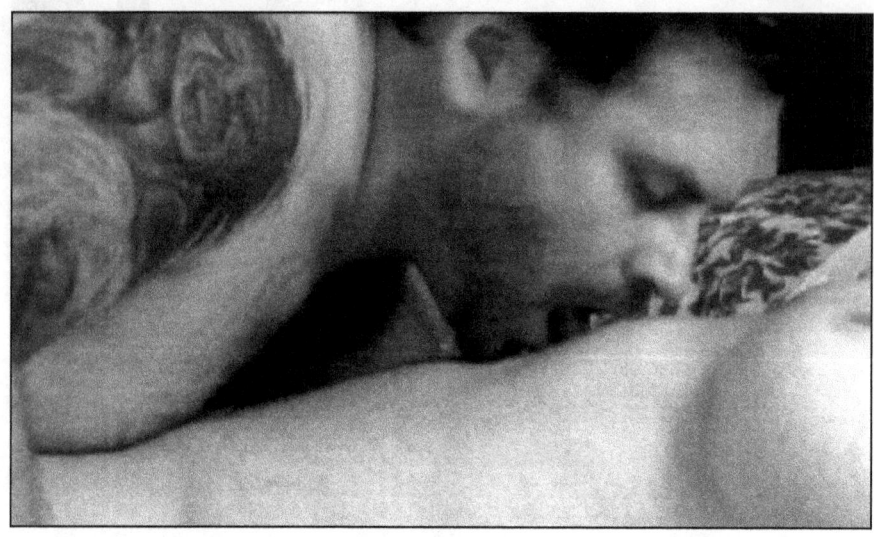

Mark plays the titular character with gusto. Photo: Baranowski Archive.

marital problem that puts him outside the law and beyond family redemption.

Given that the movie opens with Ryli getting coke snorted off her backside, and that she then reciprocates on Mark's—well, not the gun he carries in a holster—you know you're in for a wild ride.

Before long, former Playboy Playmate/adult film actress Teri Weigel shows up as a prostitute (part of a ring run by the detective); it's revealed that Mark is sleeping with his sister-in-law; and his teen daughter is having knock-down-drag-outs with her mom.

Ryli and Mark prepare for the "coke-on-dick" scene. Photo: Baranowski Archive.

Kelly Shibari and Teri Weigel—moneymakers! Photo courtesy of Murrill Maglio/Baranowski Archive.

Prince of the City, Mark is not. He is less running things than they are running him. With a contract out on his life, and his own partner on the force (and in crime, as well) proved to be untrustworthy, it's just a matter of time until it all crashes down.

This is one of Mark's riskiest movies in terms of the degree of immoral behavior to which his characters descend, and it's also one of his

Demond Reed as Mark's equally corrupt partner. Photo: Baranowski Archive.

most observational. We don't so much identify with the characters as we stand back and study them. It's an approach he'd just used in *Ill Times*, a companion piece of sorts.

MB: With money still left over from the tax credit, and a hefty bonus from the day job, I was determined to make up for lost time. Immediately following the release of *Ill Times*, I started writing another script for a film that I would end up completing by the year's end. Most importantly, I was no longer obsessed with filmmaking, nor did I lose sight of the most important thing in my life—my family. The acting bug had even begun to bite Ryli again, and she was ready to bring her alter ego out from retirement.

And what a return it was… The opening scene revealed me snorting cocaine (coffee creamer, actually) off of her naked behind, to which she responds in kind with my erect penis. Patrick Keenan, one of our co-stars (fresh off his scene with Sandra Bullock in *The Blind Side*), affectionately called it the "coke-on-dick" scene.

Needless to say, I greatly enjoyed making *Mister Dissolute*. Although it only contributed to my still-lingering credit card debt, both the experi-

Ryli and Mark, hard at work. Photo: Baranowski Archive.

ence and the opportunity to work with people I'd been a fan of for years was worth every penny. Every weekend for nearly two months, a new actress flew into Charlotte and stayed with us: Ashlie Rhey; Janet Keijser; Sofiya Smirnova; Anna Engels; Kelly Shibari; and Suzi Lorraine. Teri Weigel and her husband, Murrill, stayed in the hotel room where my love scene with Ryli took place. Maria Kil drove in from Tennessee with her family, and then headed back home to Florida after her scenes wrapped.

Another out-of-town actress who at least had less distance to travel (from Columbia, South Carolina) was Ellen Rodillo-Fowler, who did a tremendous job playing my character's frazzled lawyer. For her final scene, she had to throw her telephone across the room after screaming

Patrick G. Keenan eyes Mark with caution. Photo: Baranowski Archive.

The lovely Maria Kil. Photo: Baranowski Archive.

The cold shoulder? Looks pretty hot to us, Maria.... Photo: Baranowski Archive.

Ellen and Mark. Photo: Baranowski Archive.

into it. Little did she know, her phone quick-dialed a pizzeria upon hitting the floor, giving the person on the other end some first-hand insight into the makings of an independent film.

Mister Blue returned, along with Demond Reed, who recommended a friend—Joseph Bey—as a last-minute replacement for a co-worker who

Mister Blue, Mark, Demond Reed. Photo: Baranowski Archive.

Phillip lines up the kill shot. Photo: Baranowski Archive.

decided he'd rather spend the afternoon washing his car. Even Ryli's nephew, Josh, nabbed a brief role as a private investigator. Rounding out the cast was Phillip Smith, a not-quite-local actor from Shelby, North Carolina. He made the hour-long drive to Charlotte just to play a silent hit man, in one brief but integral scene.

Being a stand-up comedienne as well as an actress, Ashlie rather surprised me with her overall seriousness when working, especially upon discovering the camera was rolling during a practice take. I was perfectly satisfied with her performance and ready to move on, but she insisted—quite heatedly—that we do it over. Apart from this incident, she was wonderful.

Ashlie Rhey examines the evidence. Photo: Baranowski Archive.

Ashlie and Mark. Photo: Baranowski Archive.

The character of Sal, the police informant, was originally written for a male. When she arrived the night before the shoot, Suzi believed this still to be the case. However, after reading the script, Janet had found Sal to be the character she most wanted to play. She convinced me to give her the part before I could reach Suzi and get her thoughts on changing the sex of the person she would share all her scenes with. Upon finding out,

Janet Keijser as the street smart "Sal". Photo: Baranowski Archive.

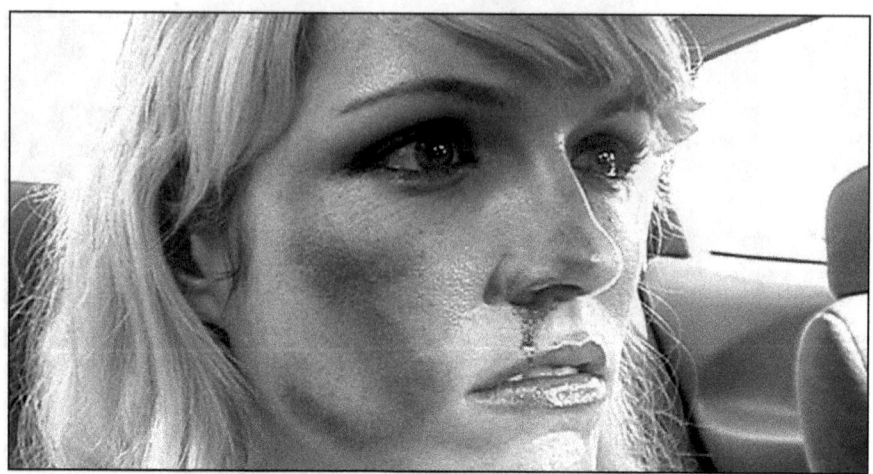

Bruised and battered: Suzi Lorraine. Photo: Baranowski Archive.

she had strong doubts, thinking there wouldn't be the right chemistry between two females to make their scenes believable. However, once she met Janet and the two began working together, Suzi changed her tune completely. It became impossible—for both Suzi and myself—to imagine anyone else playing Sal but Janet.

Angelic Anna. Photo: Baranowski Archive.

Anna was a fairly inexperienced actress, but she was a natural. Referred to me by director-actor Donald Farmer, she not only memorized all of her lines, she delivered them like a seasoned professional. I'll be forever grateful to Donald for the connection. In Anna's own words, she was drawn to play the part of my daughter because there was little "acting" for her to do; the script paralleled that of her relationship with her own father. The poor girl.

Sofiya Smirnova. Photo: Baranowski Archive.

Kelly Shibari. Photo: Baranowski Archive.

Kelly and Teri. Photo: Baranowski Archive.

"Mister Dissolute" himself. Photo: Baranowski Archive.

Poster and DVD box cover art. Photo: Baranowski Archive.

11

Hardly Beloved

Release date: November 1, 2011
Director: Mark Baranowski
Writer: Mark Baranowski
Producer: Mark Baranowski
Music: MARQUIS (Mark Baranowski), Dreamkiller
Genre: Drama
Runtime: 82 minutes
Cast: Mark Baranowski, Teri Weigel, Michael Hicks, Ryli Morgan, Patrick G. Keenan, Suzi Lorraine, Todd Brown, Vanelle, Mister Blue, Christy Johnson, Dennis Cothran, Anna Nalepka, Hooda, Rachelle Williams, Ellen Rodillo-Fowler, Todd Bagley, Eryk Baranowski, Kristin Jann-Fischer, Tony Kelley
Plot: Frustrated by his promiscuous wife, and haunted by memories of an abusive stepfather, Chad's self-esteem is at an all-time low. A psychiatrist attempts to help rid him of his feelings of inadequacy, but Chad soon realizes that only he himself can bring about a change for the better. Of course, nothing worthwhile is ever easy... To leave the past behind, take charge of his life, and become a more dedicated husband and father, he'll need to face certain challenges and confrontations head on—ready or not!

SKB: Most filmmakers drop hints about themselves in their movies. Their choice of material alone tells you a lot about what they value, and what they are afraid of. Anyone paying attention to Woody Allen's movies

Mark bravely faces his demons. Photo: Baranowski Archive.

could have told you he would hook up with a much younger woman long before it happened (*Manhattan*, anyone?).

For Mark, *Hardly Beloved* is his most confessional movie. Stripped of subplots about supernatural happenings, or violent drug deals, the steer-

Michael Hicks as the cruel, domineering stepfather. Photo: Baranowski Archive.

ing wind for the story is Mark's character and his problems with his past. And as we all discover in our own lives, the past inevitably corrupts the present, pouring into the crevices and ensuring that each day is stained with incidents from years ago.

In sections, *Hardly Beloved* resembles a European sex comedy, with scenes of Teri Weigel and Ryli frolicking together. But the main thrust is the inability of Mark's character to make sense of, and take control of, his life. His fractured relationships with his father, stepfather, cousin, and other family members (as well as friends that make characters in a Beckett play seem normal), keep him frozen in place.

As he stands on the sidelines and watches his life whirl around him, he attempts to deal with how he got into this mess (thanks to a sexy therapist, played by Vanelle).

Though the going is bleak in many ways, there are moments of dark humor. The amigos who congregate in Mark's backyard seem to have an affinity for getting into confrontations (staged more like a clown fight at a circus than a serious beat down), and Rachelle Williams shows up as a crazy hitchhiker with a switchblade, reminding Mark that random encounters with women are definitely not good for his mental or physical health.

Throughout, Mark is in Nick Hornby territory, and the emphasis on the broken circle of family ties leads to a coda that shows him reconnecting with his stepfather, who apologizes for the way he treated the family, two decades before.

Ryli and Teri, at play. Photo: Baranowski Archive.

The breathtakingly seductive Vanelle: not your average shrink!
Photo: Baranowski Archive.

Not totally a happy ending… but there is a final sense of peace that was not even hinted at in *Despair*. Maturity—even for filmmakers—brings with it not only a better understanding of ourselves, but a re-prioritization that allows us to view the past, the present, and what we hope will be our future, with greater clarity.

Rachelle lights up Mark's life…. Photo: Baranowski Archive.

Michael, Eryk, and Mark. Photo: Baranowski Archive.

MB: In early 2010, less than two months after the release of *Mister Dissolute*, Ryli became pregnant with our second child, Sara. I'd already tired of the filmmaking process, and had started the rumor that I would pick up my camera no more. No one believed it. I insisted, especially since I'd begun to see life as a series of "missed shots" whenever my camera wasn't with me. I'd become unsatisfied with simply living and appreciating life; I had to record it.

Sara was born in September, and for a few months, it was easy to stand by my claim of retirement. With a house and a growing family, I had neither the time or finances to make another film, even if I wanted to. On the other hand, I'd been planning to write an autobiography in order to exorcize some negative childhood memories, and to face certain personal issues head-on.

It was just taking too long.

Finally, I decided that one more film was in order. I transferred what I'd written for the book into screenplay format, added some fictional material to tie it all together, and began casting my most cathartic project to date.

For the most part, I chose to bring back actors I'd worked with before, and was comfortable with. It was especially important to me that the characters be played just as I remembered the actual people they were based on, and I had no doubt that these talented folks could deliver.

Patrick G. Keenan… Hardly Father-of-the-Year. Photo: Baranowski Archive.

By that point, Teri Weigel was just like family anyway, so it felt most natural to cast her as my wife (having Ryli play the part would have made things too uncomfortably realistic). I hadn't intended to have Michael Hicks portray my stepfather, but since he insisted he could do the character justice, I gave him a shot. He played it perfectly, and I commend him

Teri and Mark get cozy. Photo: Baranowski Archive.

Hooda, Mark, Ellen Rodillo-Fowler, Dennis Cothran, Mister Blue.
Photo: Baranowski Archive.

for not backing down so someone else could play the part.

The faces that were new to an "On Mark Production" belonged either to people I'd wanted to work with for years (such as Vanelle and Anna Nalepka), or who came highly recommended: Todd Bagley; Kristin Jann-Fischer; Hooda; and Christy Johnson. All proved to be well worth the wait, and lived up to their recommendations, to say the least. Christy

Todd Brown, Mark, Christy Johnson. Photo: Baranowski Archive.

brought along an added bonus (as Todd Brown and Travis Lakeman did, for *Ill Times*), being the lead singer for the band Dreamkiller. Their songs make up a large portion of the *Hardly Beloved* soundtrack.

I was especially proud to have Eryk play the dual roles of "Eryk" and "Young Chad." As the former, he was just being himself, delivering his own dialogue. As the latter, he was being me, when I was his age... At least he was spared the consequences of his actions, unlike I was.

I sent a finished copy of the film to Lawrence Toppman, and once more, I made the Sunday edition of *The Charlotte Observer*. The article discussed my father (the main catalyst for *Hardly Beloved*), the film it-

Eryk, precocious son of Mark and Ryli. Photo: Baranowski Archive.

Mark with Anna Nalepka. Photo: Baranowski Archive.

self, and my apparent farewell to the form. Soon after it hit newsstands, I heard from two local Christians who'd publicly criticized me, ten years earlier, for "making pornography." One apologized. The other praised me

Suzi, Eryk, and Ryli. Photo: Baranowski Archive.

for how far I'd come in ten years. Both revealed that, although they would never admit it to anyone else, they owned and enjoyed every one of my "provocative" films.

If I did nothing else in ten years, at least I loosened the Bible Belt a notch. My work here is done. Consider this book a celebration of not only my efforts and Ryli's, but of all those who came along for the ride (in no particular order): actors; press; co-workers; friends; family (except my own, who just didn't "get it"); location providers; general supporters; Scott Barker; Douglas Waltz. Thank you, everyone. You mean the world to me.

Now, to pay off this last credit card....

Mark with Tony Kelley. Photo: Baranowski Archive.

Mark with Kristin Jann-Fischer. Photo: Baranowski Archive.

Mark with Suzi Lorraine. Photo: Baranowski Archive.

Patrick G. Keenan and Mark. Photo: Baranowski Archive.

Mark with Todd Bagley. Photo: Baranowski Archive.

Mark with Vanelle. Photo: Baranowski Archive.

Rachelle, Mark, Ryli. Photo: Baranowski Archive.

Appendix One

Hardly Beloved shooting script

HARDLY BELOVED

by

Mark Baranowski

FADE IN:

EXT. PARK – DAY

LA WS of sky, treetops.

> DANIELLE (V.O.)
> What a beautiful sky... So vast... So peaceful...
> So unfair. It hangs over us, taunting, beckoning...
> offering an escape we can never have...
> Fucking gravity.
> We're stuck here on the ground, forced to
> accept, to assimilate, to make the most of
> our lives and to do unto others as we would
> have done unto ourselves. But, it's all good...

HA CU of DANIELLE, lying face-up on the grass, her hands behind her head. She grins devilishly.

                    DANIELLE
                  (to the camera)
        ...'cause we're some masochistic motherfuckers.

CUT TO:

INT. BATHROOM – DAY

CU of BUZZ, reclined in the bathtub, surrounded by bubbles. His face is concealed with the *Draculina* magazine he's reading. A beat, then he lowers it, addresses the camera.

                      BUZZ
           Yup... it's one of <u>those</u> kinda movies.

He suddenly lunges forward, SHOUTS furiously.

                      BUZZ
              SO GO TO BED, GRANDMA!

CUT TO:

EXT. CHAD'S BACKYARD – SHED – DAY

ECU of padlock – as it's unlocked.

ECU of door handle – as it's turned, pulled.

INT. SHED

LA CU of fluorescent lights – as they flicker on.

ECU of door – as it's pulled closed, the handle turned and a broom handle slid behind it.

LA ECU of top slide bolt – as it's thrown into place.

HA ECU of bottom slide bolt – as it's thrown into place.

CU of CYNTHIA and SUZANNE – from beside them – as they collide into a passionate kiss. Their hands explore each other frantically – along their faces, down their bodies. Necks are tongued and kissed, hair is pulled, clothes are torn off in a frenzy and thrown to the floor.

                    SUZANNE
            (breathless, between kisses)
        Why do we have to do this in here?

                    CYNTHIA
              'Cause it's the–
                    (kiss)
        one place that my husband–
                    (kiss)
            wouldn't think to look.

                    SUZANNE
                    (gasps)
                      Oh…

She smiles, GASPS once again with sheer pleasure as Cynthia kisses her breasts and continues downward – out of frame. Suzanne throws her head back, smiles as she runs her fingers through her hair.

EXT. SHED

CU of a forlorn CHAD – leaned against the door, listening to the women's MOANS from within. After a beat, he turns away, shaking his head – exits frame.

CUT TO:

INT. CHAD'S HOUSE – BATHROOM – DAY

CU of toilet – as Chad enters frame, sits on the lid and dials his cell phone with a pout.

CUT TO:

EXT. JOE'S HOUSE – BACKYARD – DAY

CU of JOE, reclined shirtless on a lounge chair. His cell phone RINGS and he frowns, opens his eyes. He picks up the phone from the ground, eyes it with irritation.

> JOE
> Oh, what the fuck do _you_ want?
> (into the phone)
> Yeah.

INT. CHAD'S BATHROOM

> CHAD
> (awkwardly)
> Hey, Dad… Got a minute?

EXT. JOE'S BACKYARD

> JOE
> (sighs)
> For _you_, anytime, son… What's up?

INT. CHAD'S BATHROOM

> CHAD
> Cynthia's having sex with another woman in our shed.

EXT. JOE'S BACKYARD

A beat. Joe doesn't move.

> JOE
> (confused)
> And… you're calling me. Weren't you invited?

INT. CHAD'S BATHROOM

                           CHAD
                       (exasperated)
            No, Dad! That's the problem! What should I do?

EXT. JOE'S BACKYARD

                            JOE
                         (angrily)
            Be a man and crash their party! Cynthia's your
               wife, for chrissakes! If she wants to add a
                 woman to the mix, you're entitled to be
              there to lick the batter! If you need _me_ to
                    tell you that, you're hopeless!

He hangs up, shakes his head and eases back into sunbathing position.

                            JOE
                        (grumbling)
                    So _what_ else is new…?

INT. CHAD'S BATHROOM

Chad closes his eyes, grimaces, SIGHS as he hangs up the phone. After a beat, he slowly rises, exits frame.

EXT. CHAD'S BACKYARD – SHED

CU of Chad as he enters frame, stands outside the door. He raises his hand to knock, hesitates – then lowers his hand.

                           CHAD
                         Cynthia?

A beat. No response from within.

                           CHAD
              I know you're in there… and I know what
                         you're doing.

                    CYNTHIA (O.S.)
               You don't know anything, Chad! Go away!

Chad frowns, frustrated.

                         CHAD
                 You're wrong! I know a lot!

He opens his mouth to continue, hesitates. A beat, then –

                         CHAD
                        Can I...?

Cynthia lets out a sudden, loud MOAN and he jumps slightly, stops. He shakes his head in embarrassment, turns away and exits frame.

CUT TO:

INT. CHAD'S HOUSE – DEN – DAY

CU of Chad – as he enters frame, sits on the couch. He stares straight ahead miserably for a beat, then picks up his cell phone, dials.

CUT TO:

EXT. PARK – DAY

CU of Chad's cousin, DANIELLE – as she YELLS impatiently.

                       DANIELLE
             Eryk, I brought you to the park to run around
                    and play! What's the problem?

HA WS of Eryk, from her POV. He sits on the grass, sticking out his bottom lip stubbornly.

                         ERYK
              You're the problem! Bad guy! You've got nuts
                          in your udders!

PREV CU of Danielle – as her cell phone RINGS. She stares at Eryk dumbly.

>   DANIELLE
>   (to herself)
>   What does that even <u>mean</u>? I give up. I swear…
>   (into the phone)
>   Hello?

INT. CHAD'S DEN

CHAD
Hey, cuz. How's your day out with Eryk goin'?

EXT. PARK

>   DANIELLE
>   I won't even answer that. This kid is unbelievable!

>   ERYK (O.S.)
>   Look, I'm holding my penis!

Danielle SIGHS, looks away.

>   DANIELLE
>   I think he's been around your dad too long.
>   My God… Anyway, what's up?

INT. CHAD'S DEN

>   CHAD
>   I need some advice. You think I should have
>   an affair?

EXT. PARK

Danielle says nothing for a beat – only squints, frowns.

ERYK (O.S.)
You're Butt Girl and I'm Penis Boy! Butter udders!

DANIELLE
Absolutely not. Keep your hands in your pockets and your zipper zipped up. The risk of you getting someone else pregnant makes me wanna bury myself alive.

INT. CHAD'S DEN

A beat. Chad says nothing, until –

CHAD
Well, <u>damn</u>.

EXT. PARK

DANIELLE
Sorry. Why do you ask?

INT. CHAD'S DEN

CHAD
Cynthia's in our shed right now, with another woman.

EXT. PARK

DANIELLE
(perplexed)
So? What are they doing?

INT. CHAD'S DEN

CHAD
(incredulous)
Well, they're not admiring my garden tool

collection! Whaddya think they're doing?

EXT. PARK

Danielle GASPS in horror.

>   DANIELLE
>   That bitch!
>   (lowers the phone, to herself)
>   I thought our time together meant something!

INT. CHAD'S DEN

>   CHAD
>   What?

EXT. PARK

>   DANIELLE
>   (into phone)
>   Nothing. You know what…? Yes. By all means.
>   Get yourself a mistress. Better yet, get three.
>   You deserve it.

INT. CHAD'S DEN

Chad ponders this for a beat – then smiles, nods.

>   CHAD
>   I think I will. Thanks, Danielle!

EXT. PARK

>   DANIELLE
>   Don't mention it.
>   (sarcastic)
>   Now let me go so I can have some more fun
>   with your son.

She hangs up, turns to Eryk.

> ERYK (O.S.)
> Bitch! Bitch! Bitch!

She drops her shoulders, closes her eyes and shakes her head.

> DANIELLE
> Lovely.

WS of Eryk, running wildly in a circle, YELLING.

> ERYK
> Bitch! Bitch! Bitch!

> DANIELLE (O.S.)
> Well, at least you're running around.

CUT TO:

ON BLACK

ONE MONTH LATER

CUT TO:

EXT. OFFICE BUILDING – DAY

CUT TO:

INT. PSYCHIATRIST'S OFFICE – DAY

CU of DR. JANE LEE – well dressed, elegant and seated cross–legged in a plush, upholstered chair. She writes in a notepad rested on her leg.

> JANE
> Okay, Chad, since this is our first session together, why don't you start by telling me about your childhood?

HA CU of Chad – seated at one end of a couch, clutching a throw pillow. With dark circles around his eyes and a haggard expression, he looks in dire need of sleep.

> CHAD
> (dazedly)
> My childhood? Yeah… The past molds us into what we are today, right? Makes sense to start there. Let's see… How far back can I remember…?

DISSOLVE TO:

FLASHBACK

INT. APARTMENT – DAY

CU of hallway – YOUNG CHAD'S POV. The camera advances slowly, turns to reveal an open BEDROOM. Someone lies sound asleep in bed.

> CHAD (V.O.)
> My first memory is waking up early on a Saturday morning and sneaking through the house, to the kitchen. It was just me and my mother, then. She was still asleep.

The camera moves from the hallway to the KITCHEN – to a drawer.

> CHAD (V.O. – CONT'D)
> It was kinda like HALLOWEEN… Instead of Michael Myers taking a knife out of the drawer, though, here was evil little Chad, pulling out a big black permanent marker.

A small hand reaches out, pulls open the drawer, extracts a large black marker and holds it up as if Young Chad is inspecting it.

> CHAD (V.O. – CONT'D)
> I was just learning to write. My name was

>   about all I could accomplish legibly... I was
>   so <u>proud</u> to be able to write my own name...
>   So I did it as much as I could, <u>wherever</u> I could.

The camera has moved on to the LIVING ROOM, behind a chair, to the wall. Young Chad's hands reappear, uncap the marker, move it toward the wall.

ECU of marker – as it enters frame, writes on the wall, just off screen.

INT. APARTMENT – YOUNG CHAD'S BEDROOM – DAY

The camera moves from the doorway to the bed. The covers are thrown aside, the uncapped marker brought back into view. It advances toward the side of the mattress.

CU of Young Chad's midsection – as he commences with writing on the mattress.

INT. APARTMENT – KITCHEN – DAY

HA ECU of the drawer, still open. The marker is placed into it, the drawer pushed closed.

>   CHAD (V.O. – CONT'D)
>   I don't know what possessed me to do it.
>   Once it was done, I forgot all about it...

FADE TO BLACK

CUT TO:

INT. APARTMENT – YOUNG CHAD'S BEDROOM – NIGHT

>   CHAD (V.O. – CONT'D)
>   ...until my soon-to-be stepfather, Barry, came
>   over that night.

LA CU of BARRY, furiously yelling into the camera – YOUNG CHAD'S POV.

> CHAD (V.O. – CONT'D)
> That whole day, my mother <u>knew</u> about the places I'd written my name, but never said anything to me about it. She told Barry instead, and let <u>him</u> dish out my punishment…
> She always did that.

Barry pulls the belt from around his waist, stretches it taut between his fists, raises it above his head – and frowns in surprise as the camera veers away, past him, into the HALLWAY. It pans backward to reveal Barry rushing from the bedroom, shouting. He runs toward the camera, which pans quickly away from him and into the next room. Suddenly, it tilts down to the floor.

END OF FLASHBACK

CUT TO:

INT. JANE'S OFFICE – DAY

ECU of Chad, staring ahead blankly.

> CHAD (CONT'D)
> I tried telling him it was my grandma that wrote my name all over the house, but he didn't believe me.
> (shrugs)
> He was the world's greatest asshole, but he wasn't stupid.

ECU of Jane. She watches Chad intently for a beat, then –

> JANE
> How badly did he punish you?

PREV ECU of Chad. He doesn't move for a beat, then he looks back at her.

CHAD
He made my mother pack up a suitcase and
threw me out on the street.

PREV ECU of Jane. She frowns in amazement.

PREV ECU of Chad. He looks at her for a beat – then shrugs, smiles.

CHAD
Of course, he called me back in, a few
minutes later. The lesson, as I recall, was
to always tell the truth, and to apologize.

PREV ECU of Jane. She shakes her head pitifully.

PREV ECU of Chad.

CHAD
There's been so many times since then that
I regretted not taking that suitcase and
keeping right on going.

JANE (O.S.)
How old were you?

CHAD
(grimaces, shrugs)
Four-ish.

CU of Jane. She shifts in her chair, takes a deep breath.

JANE
If the police had found you, they would
have taken you back, anyway... *If* you were
lucky enough to stay safe until then.

CU of Chad. He looks back at her grimly.

                        CHAD
        Doc, I'm sure any possibilities would have
           been better than how things turned out.

DISSOLVE TO:

FLASHBACKS

INT. KITCHEN – NIGHT

YOUNG CHAD'S POV – CU of Barry, seated at the kitchen table. A tape recorder rests before him. He stares at the camera with a cruel smirk, presses two buttons on the recorder.

                        BARRY
                It's recording… You ready?

The camera tilts up and down. Barry's smirk disappears.

                        BARRY
                      (hostile)
        Hey, Polack, you have to <u>speak</u> to be recorded!
                  Get with the program!
                      (relaxes)
           Now where'd you get the toy that you took
            to school today? Your mama didn't buy it
             for you, so you musta swiped it from
                    somewhere… Where?

The camera moves to the right.

                    BARRY (O.S.)
            Don't look over there, look at me!

The camera quickly moves back to Barry. He points a threatening finger at it.

                        BARRY
            Do that one more time, and I'll tan your
              fuckin' hide, you understand me?

                    (a beat, louder)
                DO YOU UNDERSTAND ME?

                    YOUNG CHAD (O.S.)
                    (whimpering)
                        Yes.

                         BARRY
            Oh, what, you're gonna <u>cry</u> now? You want me
                to tell everybody you're a crybaby?
                    (mimicking Chad)
                Little Chad's a crybaby...

The camera suddenly moves away from the table. Barry turns serious, starts to get up.

                         BARRY
            Hey, where <u>you</u> goin'? Sit down!

The camera moves away, towards the next room, back to Barry – who follows with eyes ablaze – and away again, advancing faster.

                      BARRY (O.S.)
                       (bellowing)
                  CHAD, GET BACK HERE!

DISSOLVE TO:

INT. HALLWAY – DAY

YOUNG CHAD'S POV – ECU of wall. After a beat, the camera moves up to a LA CU of Barry. He glares down at it, his hands on his hips.

                         BARRY
                       (shouting)
            Don't look at me, look at the wall!

The camera moves back to the wall.

> BARRY (O.S.)
> Keep your eyes on that spot, right there--

His hand enters frame, points to a miniscule speck on the wall.

> BARRY (O.S. – CONT'D)
> --and don't you move 'em, or close 'em!
> If I come back in here and find you asleep
> or lookin' at somethin' else, you'll get the
> belt again, understand?

The camera tilts slowly up and down. Barry flips it the middle finger before his hand exits frame.

DISSOLVE TO:

INT. LIVING ROOM – DAY

YOUNG CHAD'S POV – CU of Barry on the couch, playfully sparring with the camera.

> BARRY
> (taunting)
> Come on, whaddya got? You want some of
> this? I don't think so!

He quickly swats at each side of the frame.

> BARRY (CONT'D)
> Ya little bitch, you can't fight! You must
> be outta your mind!

The camera suddenly advances toward him, throwing him off balance. He backs away in surprise, then shoves the camera away and angrily grabs a throw pillow.

> BARRY
> You are outta your mind, you little bastard!

The camera tilts up to follow him as he stands, glares down at it.

> BARRY (CONT'D)
> I was only playin' with you! You wanna get rough, fine!

He lunges toward the camera with the pillow in front of him, covers it.

END OF FLASHBACK

CUT TO:

INT. JANE'S OFFICE – DAY

HA CU of Jane. She leans forward, frowns at Chad with concern.

> JANE
> Wait a minute. He covered your face with a <u>pillow</u>? For how long?

HA CU of Chad.

> CHAD
> Just until I didn't move around so much. Then he took it away and went outside.
> (shrugs)
> Playtime was over.

PREV HA CU of Jane. She sits back in the chair.

> JANE
> (grimly)
> I'd hardly call that playtime. Where was your mother during all this?

PREV HA CU of Chad.

                        CHAD
                     (indifferent)
            Another room, or at the store. I don't
            remember. It's not like she wasn't aware
              of how he treated me. She just couldn't
                       be bothered.

PREV HA CU of Jane. She shakes her head solemnly. After a beat—

                        JANE
            I can only assume things grew worse as
                     you got older...?

PREV HA CU of Chad.

                        CHAD
                      (snickers)
                Yeah, something like that.

DISSOLVE TO:

FLASHBACKS

INT. GARAGE – DAY

YOUNG CHAD'S POV – CU of Barry, as he pulls horror magazines and comic books out of a cardboard box, holds them up to the camera as he RANTS.

                       BARRY
             Look what I found under your dresser while
               you were at school today! Is this what you
                spend your allowance on? <u>Garbage</u>? You like
                this trash, huh? Well, guess where it's all goin'...

He throws the books back into the box and smugly picks it up, carries it to a garbage can and drops it in. He brushes his hands together and smiles proudly at the camera.

                    BARRY (CONT'D)
                  Exactly where it belongs!

He suddenly crouches, inches toward the camera with an exaggerated pout.

                         BARRY
                       (teasing)
          Oh, what's wrong? You gonna cry now? Yep,
                    I think you are...
                       (pointing)
          Look, there's a tear, and oh, there's another one!

DISSOLVE TO:

INT. DINING ROOM – NIGHT

YOUNG CHAD'S POV – CU of Barry, as he eats his dinner.

                         BARRY
          ...And you need to get out of the house more
          often. Find some friends. Get a girlfriend.
                    (stifles a laugh)
          What am I sayin'? <u>That'll</u> be the day. Girls
          don't like nerds. Especially <u>fat</u> ones. You
          need exercise, that's your problem. Well,
          you're gonna get plenty over the next
          couple months. You're goin' to camp for two
          weeks, and then you're startin' baseball.
          And don't tell me you don't like sports.
                 You'll <u>learn</u> to like 'em...

DISSOLVE TO:

INT. LIVING ROOM – NIGHT

YOUNG CHAD'S POV – HA CU of Barry, reclined on the couch and watching TV, eating potato chips.

                    BARRY
    No, you can't watch Miami Vice. Get to bed!
       You need your rest for the baseball game
       tomorrow… as if the coach'll even let you
       play. If I'd known you'd be on the bench all
       season, I wouldn't have told your mother to
       sign you up! At least you get some exercise
         walking three miles to the park and back…

DISSOLVE TO:

INT. BATHROOM – DAY

YOUNG CHAD'S POV – WS of closed door, from the toilet. Barry
SHOUTS through the door.

                    BARRY
         What the hell you doin' in there? Stop playin'
            with yourself and get downstairs! Your
                mother's got dinner ready!

DISSOLVE TO:

EXT. DRIVEWAY – DAY

YOUNG CHAD'S POV – CU of Barry, as he slowly approaches the camera.

                    BARRY
         I don't care how old you are, or how big you
            get, you will never… ever be able to take
                        me down.

He points his finger at the camera.

                 BARRY (CONT'D)
          You're a wimp… You've always been one,
              and you always will be. You're gonna end
          up just like your father, a drunken bum, and

> even though he ain't worth shit, I don't
> blame him for wantin' nothin' to do with ya...
> Now get outta here.

He turns, starts walking away from the camera, then glances over his shoulder and stops.

> BARRY
> Get <u>outta</u> here, I said! What are you, a tough
> guy, now? You've been runnin' away from
> me all your life, and <u>now</u> you're gonna stand
> there and take it? You ain't worth the effort
> anymore! <u>Beat</u> it!

The camera moves away slowly, advances down the sidewalk.

> BARRY (O.S.)
> That's it! And hey, do me a favor, huh?
> Don't come back! Fuckin' Polack...

END OF FLASHBACKS

DISSOLVE TO:

INT. JANE'S OFFICE – DAY

ECU of Chad. With tear-filled eyes, he stares straight ahead for a beat – then smiles, looks down at his lap in slight embarrassment.

ECU of Jane. She watches him intently, solemn. After a beat–

> JANE
> (softly)
> Wow.

PREV ECU of Chad.

                    CHAD
              (chuckles)
    You know, the worst part about it... My
    mom's parents never liked Barry, but when
      she finally left him they took his side.

He looks up at Jane, grimacing hatefully.

                CHAD (CONT'D)
     They felt sorry for him. After 25 years
      of marriage, how could she just walk out...?

He shrugs, shakes his head.

                CHAD (CONT'D)
      It was too ironic... I had no reason to be
       nice to her by that point, yet I was the
              only one in her corner.
                  (a long beat)
       Is there something wrong with <u>me</u>?

ECU of Jane. Sadly, she stares back at him. After a long beat–

                    JANE
                     No.

WS of Chad, from her POV. He looks at her for a beat, then suddenly INHALES, wipes his face with his palms.

                    CHAD
              Well, that's a relief.

He looks up at the clock on the wall.

                CHAD (CONT'D)
           But, it looks like our time's up.

WS of Jane, from his POV. She caps her pen, smiles and uncrosses her legs.

>   JANE
>   That's usually _my_ line.

CU of Chad, from her POV. He eyes her curiously for a beat.

CU of Jane, from his POV. She moves to the edge of her seat, smiles with a hint of seduction.

>   JANE
>   I find you very… intriguing, Chad, and I
>   don't normally say that to my patients.
>   (a beat)
>   I look forward to our next session.

PREV CU of Chad. He ponders this with a smile for a beat, then nods.

>   CHAD
>   Me, too.

CUT TO:

EXT. CHAD'S HOUSE – NIGHT

CUT TO:

INT. CHAD'S HOUSE – BEDROOM – NIGHT

HA WS of Chad, tossing and turning in bed. He sleeps alone.

ECU of Chad – as he relaxes, but still stirs restlessly.

DISSOLVE TO:

FLASHBACK

INT. CHAD'S HOUSE – LIVING ROOM – NIGHT

CU of Chad, typing on the computer while talking on his cell phone – a Bluetooth in his ear.

CHAD
Well, it was your idea! You're saying I
shouldn't do it, now?

CUT TO:

INT. DANIELLE'S APARTMENT - BEDROOM - NIGHT

HA CU of Danielle - sitting up in bed with her back to the headboard, wearing only a flannel shirt and panties.

DANIELLE
I didn't say that. I've just had some time
to think about it, and it might not be in
your best interest.

INT. CHAD'S LIVING ROOM

PREV CU of Chad. He stops typing, looks up at the wall.

CHAD
(sighs)
If you're referring to Cynthia, I've got
nothing to worry about. Believe me.

INT. DANIELLE'S BEDROOM

CU of Danielle.

DANIELLE
Chad, she's still your wife. Running out and
doing the same thing she's been doing to you
might only backfire and cause you more
trouble than you've already got... Do you
guys still have sex?

INT. CHAD'S LIVING ROOM

PREV CU of Chad. He frowns, winces in surprise.

                    CHAD
              Uh… Yeah.

INT. DANIELLE'S BEDROOM

PREV CU of Danielle.

                  DANIELLE
        Then you can't exactly cry Alienation of
        Affection. She's not even seeing other men.

INT. CHAD'S LIVING ROOM

ECU of Chad.

                    CHAD
        And what happens when she decides to
        leave me for one of these women she's
        running around with? I should just sit
        here alone on Friday night while she's
        out doing God knows what – or who –
              in the meantime?

INT. DANIELLE'S BEDROOM

ECU of Danielle. She SIGHS, leans her head back against the headboard.

                  DANIELLE
                (a beat, quietly)
        I guess not… Just be careful, okay?

INT. CHAD'S LIVING ROOM

CU of Chad. He smiles, resumes typing.

                    CHAD
        I promise. You know, this whole Internet
        Dating thing is so much easier than the bar
        scene we grew up with. Type in what you're

looking for, and <u>bam</u>… Take your pick.

He leans forward, smiles.

CU of computer screen – ZOOM IN slowly on MIYUKI'S picture.

> CHAD (O.S.)
> And I think I've just taken mine…

DISSOLVE TO:

INT. CHAD'S CAR – DAY

ECU of MIYUKI, seated in the passenger seat – smiling demurely at the camera from the driver's side POV. She looks to the passenger door – as it's closed by Chad from the outside. She watches him as he walks around the front of the car.

CU of driver's side, from passenger side window. Chad gets in, pulls the door closed and SIGHS wearily.

> CHAD
> I'm stuffed.

CU of Miyuki, from driver's side.

> MIYUKI
> (soft-spoken)
> You're very different from my other dates, Chad.

CU of Chad, from passenger side. He looks at her with a troubled frown.

> CHAD
> Really? Is that a good thing, or…?

PREV CU of Miyuki.

                    MIYUKI
                (smiles reassuringly)
        Oh, yes. It's just that my first dates at a
        restaurant usually involve little eating and
           much talk… You were able to do both.

PREV CU of Chad. He stares, wide-eyed, at her for a beat – then snaps out of it.

                     CHAD
        Yeah… Well, I don't even know what to say
            about that. Did you enjoy your meal?

                    MIYUKI
                (nods emphatically)
                Very much, thank you.

                     CHAD
        Good. So, what would you like to do now?
        Go to a movie, walk through the park, head
                 back to my place…?

ECU of Miyuki, from his POV. She GASPS, looks at him suddenly.

                    MIYUKI
        I thought you'd never ask! I wish to go home
                    with you! Please!

ECU of Chad, from her POV. He stares at her in amazement.

                     CHAD
                 Are you serious?

                 MIYUKI (O.S.)
                      Very!

                     CHAD
                  Okay. Let's go!

He fumbles through his key ring, starts the car.

DISSOLVE TO:

INT. CHAD'S HOUSE – BEDROOM – NIGHT

MONTAGE of CU's – Miyuki slipping off her blouse with a seductive look… Chad watching her in admiration from the bed… Miyuki climbing slowly onto the bed, toward Chad, he caresses her face… Miyuki's bare back as she moves in ecstasy – runs her hands along her neck, face, through her hair… ECU of Miyuki's skin – as a bead of sweat glides down… ECU of her face, eyes, mouth, etc…

DISSOLVE TO:

INT. BEDROOM – LATER

HA CU of Miyuki, Chad on the bed – lying on their backs, sweaty, out of breath, gazing up at the ceiling.

>				MIYUKI
> I think I love you, Chad.
>
>				CHAD
> You do? That's swell.
>
>				MIYUKI
> But do you love me?
>
>				CHAD
>			(a beat, looks at her)
> Sure.

She looks back at him, smiles, caresses his face.

>				MIYUKI
> I'll be right back.

She gets up, exits frame.

WS of Miyuki – with Chad's dresser, wedding ring in the foreground – as she stands, moves toward the door. She glances at the ring lying on the dresser – and stops, frowns, advances toward it slowly, picks it up.

LA CU of Miyuki, from Chad's POV. She turns to him, frowning. She holds out the ring.

>   MIYUKI
>   What is this?

HA CU of Chad, from her POV. He stares at it for a beat, SIGHS guiltily.

>   CHAD
>   My wedding ring.

PREV LA CU of Miyuki.

>   MIYUKI
>   You're still married?

>   CHAD
>   It's not that simple. Yes, I'm married, but–

>   MIYUKI
>   (louder)
>   You lied.

>   CHAD
>   No, I just didn't tell the whole truth.
>   But, Miyuki, listen–

She suddenly throws the ring at him, SCREAMS.

>   MIYUKI
>   YOU LIED!

Chad stares at her, his eyes wide, mouth agape.

LA ECU of Miyuki. She glares back at him, tight-lipped, breathing deeply through her nose. After a beat, she storms out of frame.

WS of Chad and Miyuki – as she leaves the room, SLAMS the bathroom door O.S. Chad SIGHS, rubs his eyes.

> CHAD
> Shit.

INT. CHAD'S HOUSE – HALLWAY

WS of Chad as he emerges from the hallway, pulling on sweatpants and a t-shirt. He stops outside the bathroom door.

> CHAD
> (through the door)
> Miyuki, I'm sorry, all right?

CU of Chad. After a silent beat, he KNOCKS softly.

> CHAD
> Miyuki, please come out and talk to me.
> I'll explain everything.

INT. CHAD'S HOUSE – BATHROOM

CU of Miyuki – staring at herself in the mirror, her face tear-streaked.

> CHAD (O.S.)
> It was supposed to happen like this. I certainly
> didn't plan on going to bed with you!

She closes her eyes, lowers her head.

HA CU of her purse, on the floor by the sink. She reaches into it slowly.

> CHAD (O.S. – CONT'D)
> Don't get me wrong, it was wonderful. I
> think we really have a special... connection,
> and it'd be a shame to throw that away.

                          (a beat)
                        Don't you agree?

She pulls out a large switchblade knife, releases the blade quietly.

INT. HALLWAY

PREV CU of Chad. He stands hopefully at the door for a beat, then drops his shoulders in defeat.

                            CHAD
                  That's all I'm gonna say through the door…
                  Come out whenever you feel like it.

He shakes his head, walks slowly down the hallway, toward the living room – out of frame.

CU of bathroom doorknob – as it slowly turns. The door opens, Miyuki emerges. PAN to follow her as she shuffles down the hall, toward the living room, holding the knife at her side.

INT. LIVING ROOM

LA CU of Miyuki, as she steps into the doorway with a blank expression. She turns her head slowly.

WS of Chad, from her POV. He crouches before a hamster cage that rests on a bookshelf, softly TAPS on the glass while the small rodent within scurries about.

LA CU of Chad, from behind the glass.

                            CHAD
                    (softly, to the hamster)
                  You still love me, don't you, girl?
                        Sure you do…

Miyuki slowly appears behind him. She stares at him expressionless, stops.

LA ECU of Miyuki. She stares down at Chad for a long beat, then shifts her gaze slightly.

ECU of the hamster, through the glass – from her POV.

PREV ECU of Miyuki. After a beat, she looks back at Chad.

LA CU of Miyuki and Chad – from beside them. She raises the knife slowly above her head – handle side down. He continues to TAP softly on the glass, unaware of her presence.

LA CU of Miyuki. After a beat, she brings down the knife swiftly. O.S., Chad GRUNTS and his body hits the floor. She stares down at it for a beat, then looks back up to the cage.

PREV LA CU of Miyuki, from behind the glass. The hamster scurries in the foreground as she approaches it, removes the lid and DROPS it to the floor – never taking her eyes off the animal. A beat, then she slowly reaches inside the cage.

LA ECU of Miyuki. Small SQUEAKS are heard O.S. as she picks up the hamster. A beat, and she suddenly winces, closes her eyes, as small flecks of blood splash across her face. The SQUEAKING stops, and she slowly opens her eyes, stares expressionless at what she's done.

DISSOLVE TO:

INT. LIVING ROOM – LATER

ECU of Chad. A beat, and then he stirs, grimaces in pain and GROANS, gingerly touches the back of his head.

HA CU of Chad – as he struggles to get to his feet. TILT UP to follow as he does, just before revealing the hamster cage.

ECU of Chad – as he rises into frame, his eyes still closed. He GROANS once again, slowly opens them, looks toward the cage – and GASPS in horror.

CU of Chad, from behind the glass – which is covered with blood. Through it we see Chad staring agape at what remains of the hamster.

END OF FLASHBACK

CUT TO:

INT. CHAD'S HOUSE – BEDROOM – NIGHT

HA WS of Chad – in bed, on his back. He GASPS, his eyes snap open. He remains tensed for a beat, and then relaxes, stares at the camera in terror until his breathing slows to normal.

CUT TO:

EXT. CHAD'S HOUSE – BACKYARD – DAY

ECU of beer can – as it's POPPED open. TILT UP to follow as it's lifted, guzzled by BUZZ. He BELCHES, SIGHS happily.

>   BUZZ
> First of the day!

PAN to follow as he shuffles to a lawn chair, sits between ROSCOE and TYLER. Loud SOUL MUSIC emanates from the open shed behind them.

>   ROSCOE
>   (hyper)
> First of the day, my ass! Motherfucker, that's your sixth! And that's the sixth time you said First of the Day! Buzz, you got a problem, you know that?

>   BUZZ
>   (lazily, waves him off)
> Yo, shut up. I ain't got no problem.

>   TYLER
>   (sipping his beer)
>   I beg to differ.

CU of Buzz, from Tyler's POV. He turns to him, looking drunk and offended. A beat–

CU of Tyler, from Buzz's POV. Calmly, Tyler looks at him, raises his eyebrows – as if awaiting a confrontational response.

PREV CU of Buzz. Roscoe looks on behind him, guzzling his own beer.

>   BUZZ
>   Beg all you want, motherfucker! Check it
>   out... My name's Buzz, right? That's how
>   I'm livin'!

CU of the three men. Tyler gives him a disgusted look, shakes his head and takes another gulp of beer while Buzz reaches into the cooler beside him, pulls out another can.

>   ROSCOE
>   Tyler's just trippin' 'cause he can't hang...
>   If his girl was here, he wouldn't be drinkin'.
>   Pussy-whipped motherfucker!

He and Buzz CACKLE loudly, slap five. Tyler rolls his eyes.

>   TYLER
>   Man, <u>shut</u> up, Roscoe! Lily ain't got nothin'
>   to do with it. <u>Somebody</u> gotta drive y'all
>   drunken asses home, right? You think Chad's
>   gonna let you crash <u>here</u>?

They all look toward the house, then back at each other.

>   ALL
>   (in unison)
>   <u>Hell</u>, naw!

CU of Roscoe.

> ROSCOE
> I don't even know why I <u>hang</u> with the motherfucker.

CU of Buzz – guzzling his beer. He finishes it, BELCHES, gazes drunkenly at the camera for a beat – then looks at Roscoe.

> BUZZ
> Shit, <u>I</u> rode wit <u>you</u>.

CU of Tyler.

> TYLER
> Come on, y'all. Chad's cool, and you know it. He's <u>been</u> cool since back in junior high. <u>You</u> know all the shit he's been through. Give him a break.

CU of Buzz.

> BUZZ
> <u>That's</u> a motherfucker that need a beer or two… or twelve.

CU of Roscoe.

> ROSCOE
> How do you <u>not</u> drink after all that shit?

CU of Buzz.

> BUZZ
> (irritated)
> Man, you makin' him sound like <u>he</u> better than us! Like <u>we</u> ain't been through some shit! <u>Everybody</u> got a sad story to tell!

CU of all three men.

                    ROSCOE
                 (impatiently)
Yeah, and right now, <u>mine</u> is I'm outta beer!
                  (to Buzz)
       Pass me another can, fool!

Buzz SUCKS HIS TEETH, grabs another can from the cooler, hands it to Roscoe. Tyler looks on, smiles in amusement, shakes his head.

                    TYLER
        Y'all crazy as hell.

CUT TO:

INT. CHAD'S HOUSE – KITCHEN – DAY

CU of PUG – as he looks out the kitchen window, at the three men in the yard.

                    PUG
    We'd better get back out there soon.
     The natives are gettin' restless.

HA CU of Chad, from Pug's POV – seated on a stool, arms crossed. He grimaces.

                    CHAD
                 (annoyed)
I <u>told</u> 'em to sit in the shed and to keep the
  music down… My neighbors are gonna end up
           callin' the cops!

LA CU of Pug, from Chad's POV. He turns to Chad, leans back against the countertop.

                        PUG
            It's <u>your</u> house! Tell 'em to leave if they
                    can't respect it!

                        CHAD
            I can't do that. We've been friends for more
                        than 20 years.

                        PUG
                      (insistent)
            But you're lettin' 'em walk all over you!

Chad nods, looks away.

                        CHAD
                  Yeah… Story of my life.

CU of Pug.

                        PUG
            Man, I only work with ya… and I don't know
            you as well as <u>they</u> do. But you asked me to be
            here just 'cause you knew they were comin'
                      over, remember?

CU of Chad. Still looking away, he grimaces, nods.

                        CHAD
                       (guiltily)
                    Yeah, I remember.

PREV CU of Pug.

                        PUG
            So you <u>obviously</u> don't want 'em here, but
            you're too afraid to tell 'em that! <u>Why</u>?

WS of Chad, Pug.

CHAD
(frustrated)
I'm not afraid! I just… I don't know. I <u>need</u> people around me right now, but I… I don't trust myself, and I don't wanna piss anybody off.

PUG
What do you <u>mean</u>, you don't trust yourself?

Chad SIGHS, looks at Pug.

CU of Chad. A beat, then he looks at the floor.

CHAD
I'm seeing a shrink, who told me I owe it to myself to be honest with people and stand up to 'em if I ever want to take control of my life. She said I won't be happy until I do, and she's <u>right</u>…

WS of Chad, Pug.

CHAD (CONT'D)
…but I've got so much anger built up, that I've been carryin' around since I was… <u>four</u>… I'm afraid of what'll happen if my honesty comes out wrong.

CU of Pug.

PUG
Honesty doesn't come out wrong. So, what I'm hearin' is you've been a doormat for everybody in your life since you were four years old… Man, that's fuckin' crazy!

PREV CU of Chad, Pug.

                    PUG (CONT'D)
        Take your _life_ back, man! Go out there and
        tell those motherfuckers to take their beer and
        sit in their _own_ yard with their jungle music!

CU of Chad. He winces, furrows his brow.

                         CHAD
                 Um… that's _my_ beer.

PREV CU of Chad, Pug. Pug stares at Chad for a beat, crosses his arms, CLEARS HIS THROAT. Suddenly, he heads for the door – exits frame.

                         PUG
                    Dude, stay here.

EXT. CHAD'S BACKYARD

WS of Roscoe, Buzz, Tyler as the camera approaches them – PUG'S POV. They look toward the camera, frown curiously.

                        ROSCOE
            What's up, tattoo man? Where the hell's
             Chad? I wanna hear some more of his
                    fucked up life stories!

                         BUZZ
            Yeah, he _rude_, leavin' his guests out here to
           drink by themselves… even if it _is_ his beer!

He and Roscoe CACKLE drunkenly, slap each other five. Tyler ignores them, addresses Pug with concern.

                        TYLER
              Where _is_ Chad? Is he all right?

CU of Pug – from behind the three men. He confronts them defiantly.

                        PUG
   <u>No</u>, he ain't alright, 'cause <u>you</u> deadbeat
     fuckers are makin' him look bad in front of
      his neighbors! Did he or did he not ask you
        to sit <u>inside</u> the shed and keep the music
                    down? <u>Huh</u>?

CU of Roscoe. He stares, dumbfounded, at Pug for a beat – PAN to Buzz as he looks at him. Buzz stares at Pug with the same expression. PAN to Tyler, who frowns at Pug.

CU of Pug. He looks at all three men impatiently, throws up his hands.

                        PUG
       <u>Well</u>? Instead of bitchin' about your host,
         why not try to be some decent <u>guests</u>? Your
            mama never taught you good <u>manners</u>?

A beat, and suddenly, he's tackled by Buzz – out of frame. Roscoe jumps in, then Tyler steps into frame, looks on as Pug gets beat down. O.S., PUNCHES and KICKS are landed, Pug GROANS in pain while Buzz and Roscoe cuss him out. After a beat, Tyler looks up, toward the house.

INT. CHAD'S KITCHEN

CU of Chad, standing at the window, watching the action in horror.

EXT. CHAD'S BACKYARD

CU of Tyler. He stares back at Chad with both anger and disappointment.

INT. CHAD'S KITCHEN

WS of Tyler, from window – CHAD'S POV. Tyler walks slowly toward the house, while Roscoe and Buzz continue to pummel Pug.

WS of Chad, from doorway. He SIGHS, shakes his head, sits on the stool, gazes at the floor.

WS of Tyler, from Chad's POV – as he steps into the doorway, expressionless. He stops, stares at Chad patiently for a beat.

CU of Chad. A beat, then he looks up at Tyler sheepishly.

CU of Tyler. A beat, then–

> TYLER
> (solemnly)
> <u>You</u> need to grow up.

ECU of Chad – still looking at Tyler, his face unchanging.

ECU of Tyler.

> TYLER (CONT'D)
> <u>Be</u> a man, Chad… For once in your miserable fuckin' life.

WS of Chad, from Tyler's POV. He SIGHS, looks toward the window.

WS of Tyler, from Chad's POV. A beat, then he glances outside.

> TYLER
> At least your <u>boy</u> had the balls to step to us and speak for you…

He looks back at Chad.

> TYLER (CONT'D)
> That should be <u>you</u> out there.

CU of Chad. He crosses his arms, looks back at Tyler, grimaces.

CU of Tyler. A beat, then he starts to leave – but suddenly stops, looks back at Chad.

> TYLER
> Oh, and the reason we didn't sit <u>inside</u>

the shed...
(sourly)
It smells like stale pussy up in there. Let
that shit air out and fuck Cynthia inside
the house from now on... Damn.

ECU of Chad. He looks down at the floor, tight-lipped – nods. O.S., the back door OPENS, SLAMS shut as Tyler leaves.

LA CU of Buz and Roscoe – PUG'S POV – as they glare down at him, still kicking, cussing. A beat, then Tyler walks into frame.

TYLER
All right, that's enough.

BUZZ
(protesting)
Man, I could go another ten minutes!

ROSCOE
Yeah, I ain't even started whoopin' this fool's
ass! Get in here, shoot your shot!

Tyler suddenly grabs him by the arm.

TYLER
(firmly)
I said that's enough!

Roscoe and Buzz stop their assault on Pug, glare at Tyler.

HA CU of Pug. His face and bare arms are a bloody mess. He GROANS in agony, spits a mouthful of blood onto the ground.

PREV LA CU of the three men. Buzz takes a threatening step towards Tyler.

BUZZ
What the fuck, man?

Tyler looks him up and down in amazement.

>   TYLER
>   Really? Did you just step to me?

>   ROSCOE
>   (nervously)
>   Yo, chill! Buzz, man, cool out… Yo, Tyler,
>   man, at least tell me we gon' to whoop
>   Chad's ass now. You heard what this
>   motherfucker said…
>   (points toward the house)
>   Dude's been playin' us, man. He deserves it!

Tyler glares at him.

>   TYLER
>   No, he doesn't… Let's just go.

He looks to Buzz once more, slowly exits frame. Buzz glares after him as Roscoe throws up his hands in frustration.

>   ROSCOE
>   Come on, man. Let's go to the titty bar.

He steps quickly out of frame, then pokes his head back in to taunt Pug once more.

>   ROSCOE
>   (exaggerated)
>   Take that, motherfucker! Wit yo punk ass…

He exits frame once more. Buzz slowly follows while glaring down at Pug. Suddenly, he turns to kick him once more. Pug GROANS miserably, Buzz exits frame.

>   BUZZ (O.S.)
>   Yo, ain't no beer left, but I'm takin' this cooler!

> ROSCOE (O.S.)
> Take the stereo, too!

FADE TO BLACK

CUT TO:

EXT. SUZANNE'S HOUSE – DAY

CUT TO:

INT. SUZANNE'S HOUSE – BEDROOM – DAY

HA CU of Cynthia, Suzanne – lying together in bed, naked. Cynthia lies on her back, gazing at the ceiling, while Suzanne sleeps peacefully against her. A beat, then Cynthia looks over to Suzanne.

CU of Cynthia, from over Suzanne's shoulder. She gazes lovingly at Suzanne, caresses her cheek, smiles. A beat, then she frowns slightly, looks back up at the ceiling.

ECU of Cynthia. She parts her lips, inhales, frowns deeper while slowly exhaling.

DISSOLVE TO:

FLASHBACKS

EXT. CHAD'S HOUSE – BACKYARD – DAY

CU of Cynthia, seated on the back steps, wearing only shorts and a t-shirt. She stares sadly at the ground while Chad RANTS O.S.

> CHAD (O.S.)
> (frantic)
> I don't know what to do, Cynthia. I'm just…
> I'm <u>done</u>.

LA CU of Chad, from her POV. He paces nervously.

                    CHAD (CONT'D)
            You know, I wake up in the morning, sit on
                the edge of the bed and I think... What's
                the point? I feel like there's nothing worth
                            waking up for.

PREV CU of Cynthia. She looks up at him with hurt and surprise.

                        CYNTHIA
            Really? I'm not worth it? Eryk's not worth it?

PREV LA CU of Chad. He stops, turns to her.

                          CHAD
            What good am I to either of you? I'm hardly
            Father of the Year, and as much as I love you...

HA ECU of Cynthia – CHAD'S POV. She stares at him with dread and anticipation.

LA ECU of Chad – CYNTHIA'S POV.

                          CHAD
                       (painfully)
            ...my own lack of self-esteem makes me not
                          trust you.

CU of Cynthia. She stares at him in disbelief for a beat, then SCOFFS.

                        CYNTHIA
            I have never, and would never, cheat on you,
            Chad. I'm sorry you're depressed, and I wish
            to God there was something I could do about
            it, but you've been carrying this around your
                         whole life!

CU of Chad. He SIGHS, looks up to the sky.

> CYNTHIA (O.S. – CONT'D)
> Thanks to your parents, and your stepdad,
> you think you're better off dead!

PREV CU of Cynthia.

> CYNTHIA (CONT'D)
> I'm not gonna sit here and try to change your
> mind, 'cause I'd be wasting my breath! It's
> on you, babe…
> (stands)
> You wanna drag yourself outta this hole
> you're livin' in, great… We'll be here for
> you. But we're not waitin' forever.

She opens the back door, takes a step up.

HA CU of Chad, from Cynthia's POV.

> CHAD
> Cynthia…

LA CU of Cynthia, from Chad's POV. She stops, looks back at him, eyebrows raised.

PREV HA CU of Chad. He hesitates, SIGHS.

> CHAD
> You can do whatever you want, in the
> meantime…
> (a beat)
> Spend time with another man, if you need to.
> I just don't wanna know about it.

PREV LA CU of Cynthia.

> CYNTHIA
> I don't need another man, Chad… but I
> appreciate your permission.

(a beat, smirks)
Doesn't mean you have <u>mine</u>.

She goes into the house, closes the door behind her.

PREV HA CU of Chad. He crosses his arms, frowns.

CUT TO:

INT. CHAD'S HOUSE – LIVING ROOM – ANOTHER DAY

ECU of Cynthia – her eyes narrowed into slits.

CYNTHIA
(demanding)
Where's our son's hamster, Chad?

ECU of Chad, seated on the couch. He looks nervous.

CHAD
I <u>told</u> you! It must have gotten out!

CYNTHIA (O.S.)
I can tell when you're lying, 'cause you're
no damn good at it! Tell me the truth, Chad,
or I'll make <u>you</u> explain it to Eryk when
Danielle brings him home!

CHAD
(throws up his hands)
Okay! I had an affair.

LA CU of Cynthia, from his POV. She stares at him for a beat, expressionless, then slowly pulls up a chair, sits.

CYNTHIA
(softly)
What?

CU of Chad, from Cynthia's POV. He crosses his arms, looks at the empty hamster cage, SIGHS. A beat, then he looks back at Cynthia.

> CHAD
> After what you did with… what's her name, out in the shed, I decided to do the same with somebody else.

ECU of Cynthia. She stares at him, SCOFFS calmly.

> CYNTHIA
> You know you're insane, right?
> (a beat, shouts)
> YOU GAVE ME PERMISSION, ASSHOLE!

CU of Chad. He shifts uncomfortably, bites his lower lip.

> CYNTHIA (O.S. – CONT'D)
> And what the fuck's that got to do with the hamster? Did you stick it up her ass and lose it, or somethin'?

> CHAD
> (disgusted)
> No!
> (a beat)
> She killed it. She found out I'm married, knocked me out and cut it in half.

ECU of Cynthia. She stares at him, unmoving, for a long beat. Finally, she CHUCKLES.

ECU of Chad. He looks at her in surprise.

CU of Cynthia, from Chad's POV. Her CHUCKLES gradually become uncontrollable LAUGHTER.

CU of Chad – as Cynthia continues LAUGHING O.S.

> CHAD
> I don't think it's funny, Cynthia, and neither would Eryk!

CU of Cynthia. She suddenly turns serious, points threateningly at Chad.

> CYNTHIA
> Fuckin-A right, he wouldn't! And <u>you're</u> gonna go buy him a new hamster, right now!

CU of Chad.

> CHAD
> Fine! And what if they don't have the same kind?

CU of Cynthia.

> CYNTHIA
> Go to another store!

CU of Chad. He throws up his hands, nods.

CU of Cynthia. She stands, shakes her head at him in disgust.

> CYNTHIA
> You're pitiful… and it <u>figures</u> this would happen to you.
> (a beat)
> I hope your little fling was worth it.

She turns, exits frame as she leaves the room.

ECU of Chad. He watches her go, clenches and unclenches his jaw in frustration. A beat, then he looks back at the hamster cage, shakes his head.

END OF FLASHBACKS

DISSOLVE TO:

INT. SUZANNE'S HOUSE – BEDROOM – DAY

ECU of Cynthia – as she stares at the ceiling. A beat, then she snickers, shakes her head.

HA CU of Cynthia, Suzanne. Cynthia looks at the sleeping Suzanne once more – then snuggles closer to her, closes her eyes.

CUT TO:

EXT. CHAD'S HOUSE – DRIVEWAY – DAY

CU of JAMIE, Cynthia's nephew – from beside Chad's car. He pokes around under the hood while Chad watches nearby.

                JAMIE
Yeah, Aunt Cynthia told me you guys were havin' problems. Honestly, I was happy to hear it. I never liked you much, Chad. You're kind of a pussy... No offense.

ECU of Chad. He frowns, grimaces.

                CHAD
                (dryly)
              None taken.

LA CU of Jamie.

                JAMIE
I'm only fixin' your car for <u>her</u> sake, ya know.
In case she needs to use it.

ECU of Chad.

                CHAD
You're a hell of a <u>guy</u>, Jamie. The model nephew.

CU of both, from behind Jamie – who suddenly rises, steps directly in front of Chad, nudges Chad's forehead with his finger.

> JAMIE
> (viciously)
> You gettin' smart with me, kid? I'll make you regret the day you were <u>born</u>! How 'bout <u>that</u>, kid?

ECU of Chad, from over Jamie's shoulder.

> CHAD
> (frowning, calmly)
> I'm old enough to be your father… <u>kid</u>.
> Chill out.

ECU of Jamie, from over Chad's shoulder. He grimaces menacingly, his chin jutting forward. A beat, then he nods, points suddenly at Chad.

> JAMIE
> Whatever, man… <u>You</u> chill out.

He turns slowly, walks back to the car.

CU of Chad. He SIGHS, looks out at the street.

> CHAD
> So, you still livin' with Cynthia's dad?

> JAMIE (O.S.)
> What's it <u>to</u> ya?

Chad shrugs.

> CHAD
> Just makin' conversation.

> JAMIE (O.S.)
> Yeah, I <u>am</u>. That okay with <u>you</u>?

                    CHAD
                    Sure!
                  (a beat)
      Glad to hear you haven't burned the house
                    down.

HA CU of Jamie, from Chad's POV. He looks slowly up at Chad, scowling.

                    JAMIE
          What's <u>that</u> supposed to mean?

                  CHAD (O.S.)
   Well, from what Cynthia's told me, you're a bit
   of a firebug. Lit up her dad's shed, or somethin'
   like that. Quite the hustler, too, I hear! Pawned
   anything you got your grubby little hands on…
        Except it was always other people's stuff!

As Chad talks, Jamie slowly rises, moves closer to Chad until he's in his face again.

ECU of Chad, from beside Jamie.

                    CHAD
              (playfully, smiling)
              What <u>up</u> wit dat?

ECU of Jamie, from beside Chad. He glares at Chad, eyes bulging.

                    JAMIE
                  (hissing)
              You're <u>insane</u>.

ECU of both.

                    CHAD
                (still smiling)
                  So I'm told.

                    JAMIE
            Do you actually <u>want</u> me to beat your ass?

                    CHAD
            No, believe it or not. I <u>would</u> like you to take
            a moment to reflect on a few facts… One, I'm
            older than you. Two, I'm family. Three, I'm a
            fellow human being, and I've never done
                        you wrong.

ECU of Chad, from beside Jamie.

                    CHAD (CONT'D)
            Now, I realize your parents were only 15 when
            you came along, and your dad went to jail not
            long after that, so it may be you just don't know
            any better. But I'm here to tell ya, pal…

ECU of Jamie, from beside Chad. He glares at Chad maniacally. Chad raises his index finger at him – Jamie winces, watches it.

                    CHAD (CONT'D)
            …If you disrespect me again, especially on my
                    property, I'll <u>kill</u> you…

Jamie looks suddenly into Chad's eyes, terrified.

ECU of Chad.

                    CHAD
                  (grinning)
                    …slowly.

PREV ECU of Jamie. He stares at Chad for a beat.

                    CHAD (O.S.)
                    Got it?

Jamie begins to back away from him, nods.

CU of Chad.

> CHAD
> <u>Good</u>. Now fix the fuckin' car and get lost.
> I got somewhere to be.

He begins to walk away.

CU of Jamie. Nodding, he watches Chad go, turns back to the car and ducks under the hood, picks up a socket wrench, goes to work.

WS of Chad, from the front patio – as he approaches.

> CHAD
> (to himself)
> God <u>damn</u>, that felt good.

He exits frame, enters the house. The door SLAMS O.S.

CUT TO:

INT. CHAD'S HOUSE – DEN – DAY

WS of Danielle, as the camera approaches her – CHAD'S POV. She tiptoes out of Eryk's bedroom, glances at the camera and holds a finger to her lips as she quietly closes the door.

CU of Chad, as he approaches the bedroom, stops. Danielle enters frame, walks through it, exits on her way to the couch.

> CHAD
> (softly)
> What's goin' on?

> DANIELLE
> (softly)
> I <u>finally</u> got Eryk to sleep. I'm takin' a nap, too.

CU of couch – as Danielle enters frame, lies down, turns onto her side.

Chad brings the footrest into frame, sits beside her.

CU of Danielle.

> DANIELLE
> (wearily)
> I hate to say it, Chad, but that kid is one of the devil's minions. I know kids have a lot of energy, but <u>he's</u> just possessed. Do you and Cynthia swear around him? You should <u>hear</u> the stuff he comes out with!

LA CU of Chad, from her POV.

> CHAD
> (indifferent)
> He hears it from the movies we watch.

DANIELLE (O.S.)
Oh, great parenting, <u>dad</u>!

He frowns, offended.

CU of Danielle.

> DANIELLE
> He wants to come in the bathroom to watch me pee, and he kicked the bedroom door open when I was changing my clothes, earlier!

> CHAD (O.S.)
> (amused)
> Were you naked?

> DANIELLE
> (angrily)
> I was topless, yes! But even if I wasn't, that's just creepy! He's old enough to understand that a woman needs her privacy!

(a beat, scowls)
What's so damn funny?

LA CU of Chad, from her POV. Smiling, he shakes his head.

CHAD
That's my boy.

HA CU of Danielle, from Chad's POV. She GASPS, still scowling.

DANIELLE
Did <u>you</u> teach him that?

PREV LA CU of Chad.

CHAD
(laughs)
No! I <u>didn't</u>! It just seems like he's the manifestation of every suppressed… desire or fantasy that's ever gone through <u>my</u> head!

PREV HA CU of Danielle. She shakes her head, turns on her other side – her back to him.

DANIELLE
You're a freak, Chad, in case you were wondering.

PREV LA CU of Chad. He nods, smiles. A beat, then he rests his chin on his palm, his elbow on his knee.

CHAD
I don't understand why you're still single, Danielle. You're terrific.

PREV HA CU of Danielle. She turns to lie on her back, smiles at him and caresses his cheek.

                   DANIELLE
              Oh, you're so sweet...
                 (suddenly frowns)
           What do you want from me _now_?

                     CHAD
         Nothing! Jeez, what is it with women today?
           Can't even take a damn compliment...

Danielle SIGHS, grimaces.

                   DANIELLE
              I'm sorry. _Thank_ you.

She looks thoughtfully at the ceiling.

               DANIELLE (CONT'D)
        I don't know. I'm just not interested in a
                relationship right now.

ECU of Danielle. She looks at Chad.

               DANIELLE (CONT'D)
       It's like you and alcohol... You saw the effects
       of it with your dad and so many of your friends
       growing up, now you're wise enough to avoid it.

LA ECU of Chad. He nods solemnly.

PREV ECU of Danielle.

               DANIELLE (CONT'D)
       I see my mom and my brother, how their
        hearts get broken over and over again...
                 I don't want _that_.
                (a beat, smiles warmly)
        Besides, what would you and Eryk do if I
           couldn't come by at a moment's notice?

CU of both, from the end of the couch. Chad smiles. A beat, then he shakes his head.

> CHAD
> I don't know… I really don't.

A beat, then he leans forward, kisses her on the cheek.

ECU of both.

> CHAD
> I love ya, cousin.

> DANIELLE
> (smiles)
> I love you, too, Chad.

PREV CU of both. Chad stands, exits frame. Danielle watches him go.

> DANIELLE (CONT'D)
> Oh, and tell Jamie he can come lay with me
> when he's done with the car!

CU of Chad, behind the couch – as he stops, his smile fading. He stares at the camera for a beat, then–

> CHAD
> Not a chance.

–and exits frame.

PREV CU of Danielle. She smiles, turns on her side, closes her eyes. O.S., the outside door SLAMS shut.

CUT TO:

EXT. SUZANNE'S HOUSE – DAY

CUT TO:

INT. SUZANNE'S HOUSE – BEDROOM – DAY

WS of bed, from doorway – PETE'S POV. The door is pushed open, the camera moves toward the bed – stops at a HA CU of Cynthia, Suzanne – still asleep.

LA CU of PETE, Suzanne's husband. He stares down at the women in shock, with eyes wide and mouth agape. A beat, then–

> PETE
> (whining)
> Suz<u>anne</u>!

PREV HA CU of the women. They awake with a jump, scowl up at the camera. Cynthia's eyebrows go up in surprise and fear, while Suzanne SCOFFS, relaxes.

> SUZANNE
> (tiredly)
> What do you <u>want</u>, Pete? Get outta here!

ECU of Pete.

> PETE
> (effeminate)
> Um… the last time I checked, this was <u>my</u> bedroom, too! How <u>dare</u> you!

HA ECU of Suzanne. She half-opens her eyes, smirks.

> SUZANNE
> Like this… Get <u>outta</u> here!

ECU of Pete. He GASPS dramatically.

> PETE
> You <u>bitch</u>! Since when do you sleep with women?

PREV HA CU of the women.

                      SUZANNE
                     (snaps back)
Around the time <u>you</u> started sleeping with <u>men</u>!

Cynthia does her best to stifle a laugh.

ECU of Pete – his eyes and mouth open wide.

                        PETE
     I <u>told</u> you nothing happened that night with
                       Mitch!

PREV HA CU of the women.

                      SUZANNE
                     (bewildered)
Who the hell's Mitch? I'm talkin' about Alex
                    and Bernie!

LA CU of Pete, from their POV. He opens his mouth to reply, hesitates.

ECU of Suzanne. She raises her eyebrows, awaiting his response.

PREV LA CU of Pete. A beat, then he whirls around, storms toward the door.

                        PETE
          Do what you want. I don't care.

PREV HA of the women. They look at each other, smile and kiss while the door SLAMS shut O.S.

CUT TO:

EXT. PUG'S APARTMENT BUILDING – DAY

CUT TO:

INT. PUG'S APARTMENT – BATHROOM – DAY

CU of Pug, from over his shoulder. He stands in front of the mirror, stares at his reflection miserably. His head is bandaged, one eye covered, his other eye swollen and bruised. Band Aids are placed randomly over the rest of his face, neck and arms.

WS of his girlfriend, SHAWNA – seated on the edge of the tub, staring pitifully at Pug. She wears boy shorts and a low-cut, form-fitting tank top. Her bare legs are crossed, her hands rested at her sides, palms down on the tub.

ECU of Shawna.

> SHAWNA
> (disgusted)
> You look ridiculous.

ECU of Pug's reflection.

> PUG
> (sarcastic)
> Thanks a lot, sweetie-pie.

ECU of Shawna.

> SHAWNA
> You went out like a bitch. You didn't even get any hits in?

ECU of Pug's reflection. He SIGHS, looks up at the ceiling.

> PUG
> No, I didn't. There were two of 'em, remember? And they were black!

HA CU of Shawna, from beside Pug. She shrugs, stares at him blankly.

> SHAWNA
> (confused)
> So… you couldn't get their skin grease on your fists, or what? What the <u>fuck</u>?

LA CU of Pug, from her POV. He turns to her, rests against the sink.

> PUG
> (shouts)
> Shut up, Shawna! If you were there, you'd understand! Trust me… White guy, black guy; black guy always wins. One white guy, <u>two</u> black guys, the white guy's vanilla pudding.

ECU of Shawna. She winces, grimaces in disgust.

PREV LA CU of Pug.

> PUG (CONT'D)
> <u>You</u> know how the blacks stick together. Well, I was doin' the same thing. Chad wasn't about to go out there and stand up to 'em, so <u>I</u> had to represent the crackers.
> WHITE POWER!

He throws his fist in the air – then immediately drops it, winces in pain, touches his shoulder tenderly.

> PUG
> Ow.

HA CU of Shawna.

> SHAWNA
> You're so full of shit. What are you, a Klan member now?

> PUG (O.S.)
> Maybe!

                    SHAWNA
                (matter-of-factly)
        Then you're not <u>my</u> boyfriend, anymore.

PAN to Pug slowly as she RANTS. He shoves his hands into his pockets, looks glumly at the floor.

                SHAWNA (CONT'D)
        You're embarrassing enough as it is. <u>Look</u> at
        you! And who the hell is Chad, anyway?
        You've never mentioned him, and now you're
            gettin' your ass kicked over him?

PAN back to her.

                SHAWNA (CONT'D)
        You don't even stand up for <u>me</u> when some
        guy grabs my ass in a bar, or puts his face
                between my tits!

LA CU of Pug. He glances up at her, looks back down.

                    PUG
                  (quietly)
            You work at a strip club, Shawna.

HA CU of Shawna, from beside Pug.

                    SHAWNA
                   (screams)
                I'M A WAITRESS!

                    PUG
              (trying to man up)
              Aw come on, you love it!

                    SHAWNA
        <u>That's</u>-not-the point! And I'm not talkin'
           about the strip club! I'm talkin' about

every time I go out with <u>you</u>!

LA CU of Pug.

                PUG
            (frustrated)
Yeah well, how you think that makes <u>me</u> feel?
Do I look like such a bitch that guys think
they can do whatever they want to you and
get away with it, like I ain't even <u>there</u>? And
     where's <u>your</u> self-respect?

ECU of Shawna. She glares at Pug for a beat as he SHOUTS at her, then she looks away, tight-lipped.

         PUG (O.S. - CONT'D)
   If it bothered you at all, <u>you</u> could say
somethin' to 'em, or <u>slap</u> 'em! It's not <u>my</u> job!

She suddenly glares back at him, snaps back.

            SHAWNA
         (stubbornly)
Well, it's not <u>my</u> job to give you some, every
time you take me to dinner or buy me
somethin'! There's relationship rulebook, and if
  there was, I wouldn't read it, anyway!

LA CU of Pug, from her POV.

              PUG
I know! You'd expect me to read it <u>to</u> you!

HA CU of both. She crosses her arms, looks at the wall with a pout. He turns, leans back against the sink and looks up at the ceiling, SIGHS deeply. A long beat, then–

ECU of Shawna. She slowly, hopefully looks back at Pug.

ECU of Pug. Ashamedly, he looks down at her, smiles.

HA CU of both. She suddenly jumps up, they embrace.

> PUG
> I love you, baby.

> SHAWNA
> I love you, too, you sexy beast.

They smile at each other for a beat, then–

> PUG
> Wanna fuck?

> SHAWNA
> (scoffs)
> Did you buy me somethin'?

> PUG
> Um… Nope.

> SHAWNA
> Looks like you're jackin' it, buddy.

She brushes past him on her way out of the room – out of frame. He rests his hand on the sink, looks up at the camera in disbelief.

CUT TO:

INT. BATHROOM – DAY

CU of Buzz, sitting in the bubble-filled bathtub, guzzling a beer. He BELCHES, then–

> BUZZ
> So, you see, life has its ups and downs, and some people communicate with their fellow man better than others. As for Chad, he was

lettin' the whole speakin' up for himself
thing get to his head...

He takes another gulp from the beer can.

ECU of Buzz.

> BUZZ (CONT'D)
> Tryin' that shit out on his father might not
> have been the best idea.

He CHUCKLES deviously.

CUT TO:

INT. CHAD'S CAR – DAY

CU of Chad, from the passenger side – as he gets behind the wheel, closes the door. He sits pensively for a beat, frowning, then pulls his cell phone from his shirt pocket – dials.

CUT TO:

EXT. JOE'S HOUSE – FRONT YARD – DAY

WS of Joe, seated on the front porch, watering the lawn.

CU of Joe. His CELL PHONE, on the ground beside him, RINGS. He takes his time picking it up, glances at it.

> JOE
> (grumbling)
> Oh, <u>wonderful</u>.
> (into the phone, cheerful)
> Chad! What's up, bubba?

INT. CHAD'S CAR

PREV CU of Chad. He takes a deep breath, exhales as he speaks.

> CHAD
> (rapidly)
> Hey, Dad! I was just out drivin' around and thought I'd stop by if you're home…? How's that sound?

EXT. JOE'S HOUSE

PREV CU of Joe. He grimaces. A beat, then–

> JOE
> (reluctantly)
> Yeah, I'm home… Come on by!

INT. CHAD'S CAR

PREV CU of Chad.

> CHAD
> I'll be there in 20 minutes. Don't go anywhere!

He smiles, hangs up, takes another deep breath and starts the car.

> CHAD
> Lord, help me.

CUT TO:

MONTAGE of EXT. locations throughout the city – traffic, pedestrians, etc.

CUT TO:

INT. CHAD'S CAR – DAY

PREV CU of Chad, as he drives.

CUT TO:

EXT. JOE'S HOUSE – DRIVEWAY – DAY

WS of Chad's car – as it pulls up to the garage, stops. Chad gets out, looks around at the neighboring houses, then at Joe's house. A beat, then he makes the Sign of the Cross, SIGHS deeply, approaches the house.

CUT TO:

INT. JOE'S HOUSE – FOYER – DAY

CU of front door – as it slowly opens. Chad pokes his head inside, looks around.

            CHAD
         (cautiously)
      Dad? You in here?

Suddenly, Joe emerges from the nearest room, frowns at Chad as he pulls the door closed behind him.

             JOE
          (irritated)
   Of course I'm in here, Chad. Where else would
                I be?

Chad enters as Joe walks past the camera, out of frame.

            CHAD
          (glumly)
   Um... Outside, maybe...? In the back yard?

INT. KITCHEN

WS of Joe, from Chad's POV. He walks to the counter, pours a cup of coffee.

             JOE
           (short)
   Nope. Already worked in the yard today...
        Could have used some help.

WS of Chad, as he slowly enters the room, leans back against the wall, puts his hands in his pockets.

> CHAD
> Yeah, well… I've got my own yard to work on.

WS of Joe, from Chad's POV. He turns sharply, glares at Chad while putting sugar in his coffee.

> JOE
> If I wanted your help, I would have talked you into it. I meant the kid next door. I give him 20 bucks to help me rake the leaves, pick weeds and cut the grass. 'Course, I'd feel better givin' that money to you… You could buy Eryk some diapers. When you gonna get him potty-trained, by the way?

WS of Chad.

> CHAD
> (already losing patience)
> He knows how to use the toilet, Dad. He's usually just too busy playing to take the time.

WS of Joe – as he goes to the fridge, takes out the milk, pours some into his coffee.

> JOE
> Is he sleeping in his own bed yet, or still with you and Cynthia?

CU of Chad. He frowns, looks out the window for a beat, then back at Joe.

> CHAD
> What do you think?

CU of Joe. He looks at Chad for a beat, then takes the milk back to the fridge.

                          JOE
                 You <u>know</u> what I think.

                      CHAD (O.S.)
                      (challenging)
             Yeah, and you're right. He's still sleeping
                     with us. So what?

Joe goes back to his coffee, stirs it.

                          JOE
                         <u>So</u>…
                      (takes a sip)
             You're gonna have a hell of a time getting him
             to sleep on his own. You <u>spoiled</u> him… Not a
                         good idea.

CU of Chad. He glares at Joe for a beat, then–

                          CHAD
             Yeah, well… <u>I</u> wasn't spoiled, and look how I
             turned out. Your greatest disappointment.

Joe leans back against the counter, eyes Chad heatedly, takes another sip, puts down the cup.

                          JOE
             I suppose you're gonna blame <u>me</u> for that.

ECU of Chad.

                          CHAD
                       I <u>could</u>.

ECU of Joe.

                          JOE
                       (indifferent)
             Go <u>ahead</u>, if it makes you feel better.

ECU of Chad.

                      CHAD
I won't feel better until <u>you</u> admit you
                      fucked up.

                      JOE
                     (sternly)
Ain't gonna happen, pal… and watch your
                     <u>mouth</u>.

                      CHAD
           (suddenly seething)
I'm <u>done</u> watchin' my mouth, <u>pal</u>… especially
                    with <u>you</u>.

CU of Joe. Eyes ablaze, he says nothing for a beat, only glares at Chad – then crosses his arms, takes a deep breath.

                      JOE
          (through clenched teeth)
You wanna tell me where all <u>this</u> is comin'
                     from?

WS of Chad. He LAUGHS sardonically, begins pacing back and forth in front of the doorway.

                      CHAD
I'm not even sure where to start… <u>Daddy-O</u>.

ECU of Joe – glaring at Chad menacingly.

WS of Chad – still pacing.

                 CHAD (CONT'D)
I guess the best place would be you tellin'
Mom you're takin' out the garbage and
comin' back, what, a week later…? Or maybe
your drunk ass tellin' her you'll dance on her

grave…? How about child support? Do you even know what that is?

ECU of Chad – as he paces.

> CHAD (CONT'D)
> Fast forward a few years, we find you smackin' me around during my first weekend with you in months… Fast forward several <u>more</u> years, we don't find you at all, and <u>haven't</u> found you since, oh, around the time of that smack-down weekend!

CU of Chad – as he paces.

> CHAD (CONT'D)
> Fast forward again… I'm no longer a minor, and the long-spoken words of my grandmother ring true. You come out of the woodwork and suddenly want to be a part of my life!
> Yay for me!

WS of Chad – as he paces.

> CHAD (CONT'D)
> I move to a new state to live with you and Wife Number Four, who was a <u>real</u> catch, lemme tell ya – and <u>astoundingly</u>, more narcissistic than <u>you</u> are… And let's face it, neither one of us relished playing the Father and Son roles. We didn't know how, and we both resented trying to make it work.

ECU of Chad – as he continues pacing.

> CHAD (CONT'D)
> <u>You</u>, however, soon realized the sense of power that came with your position, and ran with it. Me, still being the loyal son,

> went along with it to avoid confrontation –
> a trick I'd mastered over the abusive years,
> thanks to ol' Barry, that shining example of
> a stepdad.

CU of Chad – as he paces.

> CHAD (CONT'D)
> Time goes on, I get my own place, I start to
> see you about as often as I did, growing up…
> Yet every visit feels like an interrogation and
> judgment of whatever decisions I've chosen
> to make on my own. I start to hate myself more
> than ever, I feel inadequate in my marriage, and
> when I <u>do</u> ask you for advice, you make me feel
> like I <u>owe</u> you something for it!

ECU of Chad. He stops pacing, frowns at Joe.

> CHAD
> I wanna ask you somethin'… You'd try to fuck
> Cynthia if you were alone with her, wouldn't you?

CU of Joe, from Chad's POV. He still has his backside to the counter, his arms crossed. He stares, expressionless, at Chad for a beat, then–

> JOE
> (shrugs)
> Sure, why not?

CU of Chad. He nods, smirks.

> CHAD
> I appreciate the honesty.
> (resumes pacing)
> You flirt with her like you're in a singles bar,
> you give her a gold necklace with a heart–
> shaped pendant when Eryk's born, and you
> walk around like Adonis with your shirt off

every time we come over... and you wonder
why we come over so seldom!

ECU of Chad – as he paces.

> CHAD (CONT'D)
> Or could it be because of this new girlfriend
> of yours? The one you bought a ring for, but
> "not because it's serious"... Is this your sudden
> attempt at a... foundation, for Eryk's sake? You
> bring her to his baptism – hell, <u>Mom</u> wasn't
> even there – and here's this woman I've never
> even <u>heard</u> about, much less <u>met</u> before!

WS of Chad – as he paces.

> CHAD (CONT'D)
> But, as always, I'm supposed to smile, be
> polite and just accept it! I mean, you're my
> <u>dad</u>... I have to <u>respect</u> you, I owe you my <u>life</u>!

CU of Chad – as he paces.

> CHAD (CONT'D)
> I'm supposed to say "Sure, Dad, I'll sell my
> house and move into <u>your</u> empty rental house
> just so you'll have good, trustworthy tenants!
> I won't home–school my son because where
> else is he gonna build character?"

ECU of Chad – pacing.

> CHAD (CONT'D)
> My mouth will hang open in awe when you
> show up in my driveway with your new
> Mercedes... I'll congratulate you to no end
> when you remind me it's been almost 30
> years since you had a drink!

WS of Chad. He stops pacing, faces Joe.

> CHAD (CONT'D)
> But will you take a genuine interest in
> <u>anything</u> that I do… In <u>anything</u> I accomplish
> that doesn't involve making money or
> screwing somebody else? Don't answer that,
> I'll do it for ya. <u>No</u>. And because of that, I
> say… <u>Fuck</u> you, Dad. <u>Fuck</u> you very much.

He turns, goes to the front door, opens it and steps outside, closes the door behind him.

WS of Joe. He remains motionless for a long beat. Finally, he takes a slow sip of coffee, goes to the table and picks up his cell phone, dials.

ECU of Joe. He clenches and unclenches his jaw, but remains expressionless. A beat, then–

> JOE
> (into phone)
> Randy, it's Joe Podosek… I need you to change
> my Will. Instead of everything going to Chad,
> have it all go to my other son, Ben… <u>Yes</u>, I'm
> sure. I'll be in to sign the new papers this
> afternoon. Thanks.

He hangs up, stares out the window for a beat. Finally, he smooths his eyebrow and shrugs, exits frame as he leaves the room.

CUT TO:

EXT. CHAD'S CAR – DAY

CU of Chad, seated behind the wheel – from outside the driver's door. He stares ahead blankly, his hands gripped tightly around the wheel. He breathes deeply for a beat, then drops his head back against the seat and lets out a hugh SIGH of relief. A beat, then he picks up his cell phone, dials.

CUT TO:

INT. SUZANNE'S HOUSE – BEDROOM – DAY

ECU of Cynthia, Suzanne – still in bed, kissing each other tenderly. A beat, then Cynthia's cell phone RINGS. She ignores it for two more RINGS then frowns, reaches for it, looks at it and answers.

> CYNTHIA
> (irritated)
> Speak, fucker.

EXT. CHAD'S CAR

PREV CU of Chad.

> CHAD
> (sternly)
> Where are you?

INT. SUZANNE'S BEDROOM

ECU of Cynthia. She cocks an eyebrow, SCOFFS.

> CYNTHIA
> Excuse me… How about, "Hi honey, how ya doin'?"

EXT. CHAD'S CAR

PREV CU of Chad.

> CHAD
> After "Speak, fucker," I should just hang up on you. If you're with Suzanne, say your goodbyes and get home. We've got lots to talk about. I'm leaving my dad's, gettin' gas and stoppin' by Tyler's. I'll be home in an hour.

He hangs up, starts the car.

WS of Joe's house, Chad's car. As Chad pulls off, out of frame, Joe strolls out onto the front porch, his hands in his pockets. He stops at the edge of the porch, sadly watches Chad go.

CUT TO:

EXT. GAS STATION – DAY

WS of parking lot. Chad's car enters frame as it pulls to a stop beside one of the pumps. Another car is parked at the curb, a short distance behind Chad's.

CU of Chad, from behind his car – as he gets out, goes to the pump. As he begins filling his tank, GRANITE calls out to him O.S.

>   GRANITE
>   (gruffly)
>   Excuse me!

Chad looks in Granite's direction curiously.

CU of GRANITE, from Chad's POV. A large, intimidating white man, he lumbers up to the camera.

>   GRANITE
> Hey, brother. My name's Granite. My wife
> and I are tryin' to get to the next county, but
> we ran outta gas. Do you have a couple dollars
>   you could spare for us to get some?

CU of Chad, from Granite's POV. He tilts to one side, looks past Granite.

PREV CU of Granite. He steps aside to reveal MONA, seated in the nearby car's passenger seat. She smirks, gives Chad a slight wave.

PREV CU of Chad. He purses his lips, shakes his head and shrugs.

                         CHAD
            I'm sorry, I don't have any cash on me.
                   (points to the pump)
              Just used a credit card for mine.

LA ECU of Granite.

                        GRANITE
                       (cheerfully)
              Well, that's okay. Money's money.

ECU of Chad. He frowns, smiles.

                         CHAD
            Um… I'm not giving you my credit card,
                   Granite. I said I'm sorry.

CU of Chad, from behind Granite. He reaches for the nozzle, slides it back onto the pump. He screws on his gas cap, smiles at Granite before getting back into the car.

                         CHAD
                      Good luck!

CU of Granite. He glares at Chad as the starts, pulls away from the pump – and then he turns, hurries back to his car.

PREV WS of the parking lot. Granite gets into his car as Chad's heads toward the driveway.

CUT TO:

INT. GRANITE'S CAR – DAY

ECU of Granite, from the backseat – as he gets behind the wheel, pulls the door closed.

                       MONA (O.S.)
                   Did you get anything?

He looks at her with determination–

>   GRANITE
>   Not <u>yet</u>, baby.

ECU of the ignition switch. His hand enters frame, turns the key.

PREV ECU of Granite.

>   GRANITE
>   (determinedly)
>   I'm gon' <u>git</u> that boy.

>   MONA (O.S.)
>   (anxious)
>   Sounds good to <u>me</u>, sugar!

He shifts gears, steps on the gas.

EXT. GAS STATION

PREV WS of parking lot. Granite's car turns around, follows Chad's as it pulls out to the street – out of frame.

CUT TO:

EXT. TYLER'S HOUSE – DAY

CUT TO:

INT. TYLER'S HOUSE – KITCHEN – DAY

CU of Tyler, leaned back against the counter, his arms crossed. His girlfriend, LILY, sits on the countertop beside him. They look at each other, snicker, as Buzz and Roscoe BICKER O.S.

>   BUZZ (O.S.)
>   (raucous)
>   Man, just tell 'em the story!

                    ROSCOE (O.S.)
                     (excitedly)
        I don't <u>feel</u> like it, man! Leave me alone!
            Yo, T, man, get me another beer!

WS of Buzz and Roscoe, from Tyler's POV – seated at the kitchen table, with empty beer bottles scattered between them.

                        BUZZ
        You don't <u>need</u> no more beer, man! Just
                    tell the story!

                       ROSCOE
        All right, all right! <u>Shit</u>! I'll tell the
                 motherfuckin' story…

Buzz grins with delight, jumps slightly out of his seat.

                        BUZZ
                       <u>Yeah</u>!
                  (to Tyler and Lily)
        Yo, check this out, he gonna tell the story!

                       ROSCOE
                   (swipes at him)
        Shut <u>up</u>, fool! I'mma tell it now!

Buzz swipes back at him playfully, relaxes. He leans forward, listens intently. Roscoe takes deep breath – and erupts with LAUGHTER.

                       ROSCOE
        PSYCHE! I ain't tellin' no fuckin' story,
              man… I'm too fuckin' drunk!

Buzz's GROANS in disappointment, waves him off.

                        BUZZ
                     (dejected)
            Aw, shit… <u>Fuck</u> you then, man!

PREV CU of Tyler, Lily. They LAUGH, look at each other and shake their heads.

> LILY
> (jokingly)
> Yeah, you're right about that, Roscoe!
> You <u>are</u> too drunk!

O.S., there comes a KNOCK at the door. She and Tyler look in its direction curiously.

WS of Buzz and Roscoe. They suddenly stop moving, talking – do the same as Lily and Tyler.

CU of Lily. She looks at the three men, CHUCKLES as she slides of the counter, walks toward the doorway – out of frame.

> LILY
> You all look like it's the cops. Don't worry,
> <u>I'll</u> get it… and I'll tell 'em you're not here.

CUT TO:

EXT. TYLER'S HOUSE – FRONT PORCH – DAY

CU of Lily – revealed as she opens the door – from over Chad's shoulder. She grins widely upon seeing him.

> LILY
> (cheerfully)
> <u>Hey</u>, Chad! Good to see you!

CU of Chad, from beside Lily. He smiles, looking a bit uncomfortable.

> CHAD
> Hey there, Lily. Uh, I need to talk to Tyler
> for a minute. Is he here?

> LILY (O.S.)
> Sure, come on in!

INT. TYLER'S KITCHEN

WS of Buzz, Roscoe.

> LILY (O.S.)
> Tyler! Chad's here to see you!

They gape at each other, at Tyler.

CU of Tyler, from their POV. He frowns, grimaces at them, looks toward the door.

PREV WS of Buzz, Roscoe. Desperately, they press their palms together, silently plead with him.

CU of Tyler. He rolls his eyes, shakes his head and looks at the floor. A beat, and then he throws up his hands.

PREV WS of Buzz, Roscoe. They bolt from their seats, out of frame.

CU of doorway. Buzz stands against one wall, Roscoe against the other – ready to pounce. Lily enters, frowns at Tyler.

> LILY
> Baby, didn't you hear me? I said Chad's here–

As Chad steps through the doorway behind her, Buzz and Roscoe tackle him simultaneously. Lily SCREAMS, jumps out of the way as they take him down.

> ROSCOE
> Gotcha, motherfucker!

> BUZZ
> Yeah, it's *your* turn, white boy!

CU of Tyler, Lily. She backs against him in horror; he comforts her while they look on – to the sound of BLOWS, KICKS O.S.

>   TYLER
>   It's all right, baby. He had it comin'.

LA CU of Buzz, Roscoe – CHAD'S POV. They look down at the camera as they punch and kick, SHOUT obscenities at it.

CUT TO:

INT. GRANITE'S CAR – DAY

CU of Granite, from the backseat.

>   GRANITE
>   (pleased)
>   <u>There</u> it is.

PAN to Chad's car, parked on the street. Granite pulls over, parks behind it.

EXT. GRANITE'S CAR

Cu of Granite, Mona – from outside the passenger door. They smirk in evil anticipation as the eye Chad's car.

>   MONA
>   He <u>couldn't</u> have parked at the curb on purpose…
>   You sure he knew we were followin' him?

Suddenly, they look toward Tyler's house in surprise as the front door BANGS open O.S.

EXT. TYLER'S HOUSE – FRONT PORCH

LA WS of the front door, hanging wide open. Buzz and Roscoe toss out a battered and bleeding Chad – he rolls off the porch and onto the sidewalk, GROANS miserably.

                    ROSCOE
        And we're <u>keepin'</u> the stereo, motherfucker!

He struts back into the house as Buzz points down at Chad.

                     BUZZ
          <u>Yeah</u>! And the <u>cooler</u>, too!

He enters the house with a swagger, SLAMS the door behind him.

EXT. GRANITE'S CAR

PREV CU of Granite, Mona. Looking down at Chad, she frowns in concern, he glares up at the house.

INT. GRANITE'S CAR

PREV CU of Granite, from the backseat. With his eyes still on the house, he turns off the car.

                    GRANITE
     Well, <u>that's</u> an interesting turn of events. You
                   comin', Mona?

                   MONA (O.S.)
                  You <u>know</u> it.

PAN to follow as he gets out, walks around the front of the car. Mona's door opens, CLOSES O.S. Through the passenger side window, we see them meet in Tyler's driveway, walk determinedly up to the front door. Granite ignores him, but Mona looks down at Chad on their way up the steps to the door. Granite KNOCKS. A beat, the door is opened – Granite shoves his way inside, followed by Mona. SHOUTS CRASHES, BLOWS are heard from within.

Chad struggles to his feet, stumbles to his car, holding his stomach – PAN to follow. Through Granite's windshield, we see him open his car door, get in.

EXT. CHAD'S CAR

WS of Tyler's house, Chad's car. Chad starts the car, drives off as the RUCKUS inside the house continues.

CUT TO:

INT. CHAD'S HOUSE – KITCHEN – DAY

CU of Cynthia, seated on a stool beside the counter. She jumps as the door BANGS open O.S.

WS of Chad, from her POV – as he stumbles into the house from outside, leans against the wall. She rushes into frame, helps him to the stool.

>   CYNTHIA
>   (frantic)
> Sweetheart, what <u>happened</u> to you? Are you
> okay? Do you need to go to the hospital?

>   CHAD
>   (weakly)
> I'm all right. Just let me sit down.

PREV CU of counter, stool – as Cynthia helps Chad sit, then rushes past him, to the bathroom.

>   CYNTHIA
> Don't move! I'll get a warm washcloth!

>   CHAD
> How about some ice?

She suddenly stops, begins running back to him –

>   CYNTHIA
> Ice? Okay... Wait!

–then stops, runs back toward the bathroom.

                    CYNTHIA
        I still need a washcloth… <u>Two</u> washcloths!

Chad forces a smile, GROANS, holds his face tenderly. Cynthia runs back to him with a washcloth in each hand – passes him on her way to the sink. O.S., the FAUCET starts running. She crosses the frame on her way to the freezer, returns with an ice tray.

                    CYNTHIA
                   (rambling)
        Okay, once the water gets warm, I'll clean
        you up with one washcloth. Then I'll put ice
        in the other one and you can hold that over
                    your eye…

Chad shifts slowly on the stool, rests both elbows on the counter, leans his face against his hands. He watches her fondly, with a slight smile.

DISSOLVE TO:

INT. CHAD'S HOUSE – DEN – LATER

CU of Cynthia, Chad – sitting together on the couch. His face and head are covered in gauze, Band Aids. His eyes are closed. Curled up next to him with her head on his shoulder, she gazes tiredly ahead. SOFT MUSIC plays O.S. A long beat, then–

                     CHAD
            What do <u>you</u> wanna do?
                   (a beat)
        Wanna get a divorce, so you can run off with
                    Suzanne?

She grimaces, SCOFFS.

                    CYNTHIA
        Are you kidding? I ain't runnin' off with no
            woman. I like <u>man</u> meat too much.

>   CHAD
>   (suggestively)
>   There are other men.

She looks up at him.

ECU of Cynthia.

>   CYNTHIA
>   Honey, chances are, another man would feel
>   like <u>this</u>, next to you…
>   (holds up her pinky finger)
>   I told you, I don't <u>need</u> another man.

She rests her head back on his shoulder.

ECU of Chad. He smiles proudly, cocks an eyebrow.

>   CHAD
>   Good to <u>know</u>.

PREV CU of Chad, Cynthia. He puts his arm around her, holds her close.

>   CHAD (CONT'D)
>   Well, in any case, things are gonna start
>   changin' around here… for the <u>better</u>.
>   (looks at her)
>   I <u>promise</u> you that.

A beat – She smiles, looks back at him.

ECU of them, gazing lovingly into each other's eyes.

>   CHAD
>   I love you.

>   CYNTHIA
>   (teary-eyed)
>   I love you too, Chad.

They kiss passionately.

DISSOLVE TO:

EXT. OFFICE BUILDING – DAY

ONE MONTH LATER

CUT TO:

INT. JANE'S OFFICE – DAY

WS of Jane, Chad, in their respective places – she in her plush chair, he on the couch. Her legs are crossed once again, the notepad on her lap. He appears much more relaxed, rested, upbeat.

                  JANE
    <u>So</u>, Chad… How've you been?

Chad smiles, nods emphatically.

                  CHAD
    I've been terrific, Doc, I have to admit. I don't
    know how much of it's me and how much is
    the medication, but the feeling of inadequacy's
    <u>gone</u>.

                  JANE
    Great! Well, keep in mind, we may have
    gotten that feeling under control, but it
    could always come back to some extent with
    hard times. It's only natural.

Chad nods.

                  CHAD
    Understood.

CU of Jane. She opens her mouth to speak, hesitates, smiles coyly.

                        JANE
              And... how are things with Cynthia?

CU of Chad, from her POV. He looks from her to the camera, smiles mischievously.

CUT TO:

FLASHBACK

INT. CHAD'S SHED – DAY

QUICK-CUT MONTAGE of CU's, ECU's – Chad, Cynthia and Suzanne kissing, caressing passionately.

END OF FLASHBACK

CUT TO:

INT. JANE'S OFFICE – DAY

CU of Chad – still smiling at the camera. A beat, then–

                        CHAD
                     (deviously)
                    Never better.

PREV CU of Jane. She nods, but with less of a smile and a hint of disappointment.

                        JANE
            That's <u>good</u>. Well... that takes care of your
                 <u>current</u> life, but what about your past?

CU of Chad. He repositions himself on the couch, rests his elbow on the arm of it, frowns and SIGHS.

                          CHAD
                       (curiously)
           What <u>about</u> it? Isn't it better to leave all
                     that behind me?

CU of Jane.

                          JANE
            In your case, Chad, I don't think so. You're
              well aware of how much one's childhood
                    can affect their adult life.
                         (a beat)
             How long's it been since you last spoke
                        with Barry?

ECU of Chad. He looks intently at Jane for a beat, then takes a deep breath, rubs his chin.

                          CHAD
                     Let's see... Uhh...
                         (a beat)
                     Twenty–two years.

ECU of Jane.

                          JANE
                  (softly, in amazement)
            Twenty–two years... You've had no contact with
              the man for <u>that</u> long, yet he's never stopped
                       controlling you.
                         (a beat)
            All you need in your life now is closure, Chad.

ECU of Chad. He stares at her for a beat with fear in his eyes, but nods slowly in agreement.

CUT TO:

EXT. AIRPORT – DAY

LA CU of airplane, as it takes off – PAN to follow.

DISSOLVE TO:

EXT. DUPLEX – DAY

WS of house, timeworn and in need of repair. ZOOM IN on it slowly.

CUT TO:

EXT. DUPLEX – FRONT DOOR – DAY

CU of doorbell. Chad's hand enters frame, presses it.

CU of door, from over Chad's shoulder. A long beat, and it's UN-LOCKED, slowly opened.

CU of Chad, in sunglasses. His mouth drops open, he slowly removes the glasses, stares in amazement.

CU of Barry's midsection – as he shuffles into the doorway, toward the camera. He wears over-sized sweatpants, a dirty t-shirt and robe. He's unshaven and looks as timeworn as the building he lives in. His eyes are dark, sunken and glassy, his thinning hair a mess. As he steps into the light, he squints, covers his eyes with a trembling hand. A beat, and his face falls upon recognizing Chad.

BARRY
(hoarsely)
It <u>can't</u> be.

PREV CU of Chad. He frowns in disbelief.

CHAD
(aghast)
<u>Barry</u>?

ECU of Barry. He drops his hand, almost smiles.

> BARRY
> I'll be damned.

ECU of Chad – as he looks Barry up and down, his eyes and mouth still agape. He slowly nods, SCOFFS.

> CHAD
> That's a safe bet.

PREV CU of door, from over Chad's shoulder. Barry shuffles up to Chad – and throws his arms around him.

CU of Chad, from behind Barry. He holds out his hands for a beat, with an even more shocked expression than he'd just worn – as Barry hugs him.

ECU of Barry. Tears roll down his face.

> BARRY
> It's so good to see you, Chad.

ECU of Chad. A long beat, as his expression gradually turns from shock to compassion. He relaxes, closes his mouth and clenches his jaw – as his eyes well up with tears.

PREV CU of Chad. A beat, and he slowly embraces Barry. His tears fall as he squeezes his eyes shut. SLO-MO as he pats Barry on the back.

DISSOLVE TO:

EXT. RIVERSIDE – DAY

WS of Chad – as he strolls toward the camera, his hands in his pockets, sunglasses on. As he walks, his focus alternates from the ground to the water, but a solemn frown remains all the while.

> CHAD (V.O.)
> Barry wouldn't let me in the house… He
> said he'd rather the outside world see him in

> his condition than subject me to the disaster area his place had become, so we stayed outside and talked... Not for long, but... long enough. After seeing him, I could understand why my grandparents felt sorry for him, though I'm not sure if he'd deteriorated to such an extent before or <u>after</u> my mom left him. She never talks about it, and I didn't have the heart to ask him... so he listened while I told him how life had treated <u>me</u> over the past 22 years. He seemed impressed, especially when I showed him a picture of Cynthia and Eryk... It made him cry. He apologized for how he'd treated me growing up, and begged me not to ever be that way to Eryk... I assured him I wouldn't.

DISSOLVE TO:

EXT. RIVERSIDE – DAY

WS of Chad – as he stands facing the water, looking out over it, head held high. ZOOM IN on him slowly.

> CHAD (V.O. – CONT'D)
> There wasn't much else to say... I'd gone there with the intention of punishing him for the years of abuse he'd put me through, but nothing I could have said or done would have amounted to the punishment he'd put <u>himself</u> through for it... I thought what I needed was revenge, or at <u>least</u> an explanation. Turned out an apology was enough... Time doesn't heal <u>all</u> wounds... Sometimes it takes a little courage.

He smiles.

FADE TO BLACK

CUT TO:

INT. BATHROOM – DAY

CU of Buzz – still in the bathtub, holding a rubber ducky above the bubbles. It SQUEAKS as he squeezes it. He smiles, then suddenly stops, looks at the camera.

> BUZZ
> Now that's how you end a movie… I know you
> liked it, grandma. Ain't you glad you ignored
> me, earlier?
> (grins, nods)
> Yeahhh…

FADE OUT.

THE END

Appendix Two

Scott Interviews Mark and Ryli

MARK

SKB: **Why the move to North Carolina from Buffalo?**

MB: My family life has never been much to speak of. I left home at fifteen and went to live with my grandparents until graduating from high school in 1992. At that point, my strongest relationship was with my girlfriend. When that fell apart a year later, I had nothing left but my job as a locksmith—a trade I could return to anywhere, if need be. In the end, it was the three feet of snowfall overnight that became the deciding factor to escape Buffalo and head to Charlotte, where my dad lived. I hardly knew him, but we were both willing to take that giant step and play our "Father" and "Son" roles for the first time in years.

SKB: **What was the biggest cultural shock for you?**

MB: Initially, the overall laid-back attitude. I can't say I experienced "Southern hospitality," because if I wasn't being called a Yankee, I was brushed aside just as I'd been by similarly self-absorbed New Yorkers. At least there wasn't the blatant animosity so prevalent in Buffalo… just simple indifference. When it came to work, it was hard not to feel a bit superior to the locals, even while I was in training. It's in my nature to give 100% to the task at hand, and to make the most of my position. To the majority of my co-workers, their job was nothing but a means to an end. The less effort they had to put forth, the better.

After more sightseeing and getting better acquainted with people, the shock came from the religious fanaticism and Bible thumping. I grew up Catholic, and never felt compelled to cram my beliefs down the throat of someone who wasn't. Nor had I ever met a Catholic who did. Down South, Christians are of a completely different mind state... one that I found terribly unnerving. I wanted nothing more than to make new friends, but the more I tried, the more alienated I became.

SKB: How did relocating help your artistic pursuits? How did it hinder them?

MB: Being separated from the family and friends I'd grown up with, and then becoming a social misfit in my new surroundings, I was left with nothing but time. Without the "distraction" of people around me, I could finally focus on potentially turning at least one of my favorite creative outlets—drawing, music and writing—from a mere hobby into a career.

If the relocation was a hindrance at all, it made my work more downbeat. I recall several bouts of depression during that lonely time, and suicide often crossed my mind. My creative outlets were my therapy, however. Without them, I would have surely acted on my darkest impulses.

SKB: What was the inspiration for *Despair*? What was production like? (What went well, what was a challenge?)

MB: The world had just experienced 9/11, and the future was looking more uncertain than ever. That was my main inspiration. On a personal level, I had quit my job and was struggling to get both my artwork and screenplays seen and sold. The bills were piling up, and my manager in Los Angeles was telling me to "be patient." The only screenwriting offers I was getting involved deferred payment, and no one with an interest in my artwork was willing to pay for it.

Production on *Despair* went quite well, actually, considering the entire process was a learning experience for Ryli and I. There was no one else involved. I wrote the script while Ryli was at work one day, and began shooting the moment she walked into our apartment, that evening. This went on for four hours, and resumed for four more, the next night. That was it. We shot the screenplay as I'd written it, from start to finish, editing in-camera along the way. The grim material hardly kept us upbeat throughout, but we managed to stay focused on getting the thing finished as soon as possible. The entire process took just under two weeks. The most challenging part was probably adding the score to the film, which I did by plugging the audio cables of a four-track recorder into a VCR that would record the synchronized playback of the film from another VCR, and the music from the recorder.

SKB: **Which film are you proudest of? Why?**

MB: My last, *Hardly Beloved*. If someone who'd never seen my films asked me which they should watch first, it'd be this one. It's my most autobiographical, and the entire cast played their roles wonderfully. It's also the one I'm most satisfied with from a technical standpoint.

SKB: **Which film was the biggest disappointment to you? Why?**

MB: Runaway Terror, our second film (third, if you count *Ryli Morgan: Audition*). I was still shooting with the VHS-C camcorder I'd used for *Despair*, and because I couldn't shoot the script in sequence, I couldn't edit in-camera. I had extremely limited funds and resources to work with. When a couple of my actors dropped out at the last minute, I was forced to rewrite the last half of the script and scrap much of the story in order to stay on schedule. The result is nearly unwatchable, as far as I'm concerned, but we were still excited to release it, at the time.

SKB: **How has your background in drawing influenced your style as a filmmaker?**

MB: I have a strong affinity for high contrast imagery, which is immediately apparent in my charcoal drawings. This naturally transferred over to my films, along with the two things I most enjoy drawing—close-ups and naked women.

SKB: **How does your music play a role in your filmmaking?**

MB: I'm often told that my music sounds "cinematic," and that it would make for a great film soundtrack. These are folks who've either never seen my films, or don't realize that each title's "Music by MARQUIS" credit refers to me. Using my own music for the soundtrack makes things so much easier, time and budget-wise, and knowing which song(s) I want to use for a certain scene during the scriptwriting process allows me to synchronize the action to coincide with the rhythm and/or lyrics. This synchronization process comes into play especially in editing, since I often enjoy cutting each frame to the beat of the music, as if creating a music video within the film.

SKB: As a filmmaker, what do you know now that you wish you knew when you started?

MB: How extremely difficult—and expensive—it is to find an appreciative audience; that you should never have friends play a part in your films unless you're willing to risk the friendship; and how so very true (and frustrating) the phrase "everyone's a critic" is.

RYLI

SKB: Was *Despair* your very first experience in front of a camera for a film? If not, what was the first? If so, what were your biggest concerns during production, and how did you deal with them?

RM: Yes, and no. My closest high school buddies and I had attempted once to put together a few scenes for a film, but it amounted to 5 minutes of us creeping around a cemetery. The footage was scrapped about a week later, when we realized we didn't have the resources necessary to match our grand ideas.

My biggest concern on *Despair*, mainly because there was little-to-no dialogue, was just hoping I could convey the necessary emotions.... Being as expressive as the content required.

SKB: How has your background as an athlete helped you as an actress?

RM: Figure skating probably helped in the area of physicality; being able to take a fall, etc. I feel it helped with expression, as well. You have to be able to show what you're feeling, since you can't talk to the crowd when you're skating.

SKB: **When did you first become interested in singing? What background/training do you have in singing? What musical genre do you feel most comfortable in?**

RM: The interest in singing started around age three or four, though I've never had any formal training. One of my earliest memories is of holding a "concert" for our neighbors, on my parents' front porch. I've always got a tune of some sort in my head, but I think I'm most akin to 1980's pop/rock (a la Pat Benatar, Laura Branigan, Stevie Nicks, etc.).

SKB: **How did your upbringing in the South help—or hinder—your work in horror films?**

RM: I'm sure it could have gone better—or worse—if I had done more auditions, or worked for more companies than I have. Considering I've remained an "in-house" actress, I didn't have to worry too much about location. Mark and I created content that we were both comfortable and happy with, at the given time. I think our location hindered us a bit, as far as how our work has been accepted. It didn't take us long to discover that T and A content isn't something that most around here admit to watching.

SKB: **What was your favorite movie as a child? As a teen? Now?**

RM: As a child, *Grease*. I wanted to be "good" Sandy. As a teen, *The Neverending Story*. Still *Grease*, too, but by then I wanted to be "bad" Sandy. Now? Ugh, that's more difficult. I'd have to actually reach back a few years, and choose something like *The Crow*—something with a meaning behind the darkness.

SKB: **What style of film that you haven't done yet would you most want to undertake?**

RM: I'd love to work on a film that's comedy from start to finish. Even a period piece would be fun, with all the costumes. I'd also like to do an all-out horror film. We've sort of been adopted by the horror genre because our thrillers tend to be a bit bloody, but we've not actually done a horror film, as of yet.

SKB: **Which of your movies are you the happiest with? Why?**

RM: I think I'm happiest with *Expendable* and *Heaven Help Me, I'm in Love*, because they came out closest to how we originally saw the story forming. It's nice to not have to make many changes along the way.

SKB: **Which of your movies would you want to do over, and why?**

RM: My choice wouldn't be so much a "do-over" as much as it would be a "new beginning". We began a film in 2003 called *The Zombie Room*. There were issues along the way with casting, unexpected weather conditions, etc., so it was sidelined. I would really love to be able to begin again on that one.

SKB: **How do you balance the dual "realities" of Scream Queen and wife/mom?**

RM: That's the best perk of being an in-house actress. I get to be Mama on a daily basis, and when Mark is ready to film something, I'm there for the project. I have fun photo sessions from time to time, as well, to kind of keep one foot in Performance mode.

SKB: **What advice would you give to young women who want to have a career in horror?**

RM: Most importantly, never do anything you're uncomfortable with. People have limits, and they should be respected. Also, don't ever let anyone tell you what you can and cannot do. Speak up for yourself. Be original. Don't let anyone try to make you out to be "the next so-and-so". Be the best YOU that you can be.

SKB: **How have your films been received in your home state?**

RM: Again, due to the level of nudity that we're comfortable with, it seems our films have been sort of swept under the rug. Or hidden under the mattress, as the case may be. It surprises me, at times when we speak of our films, even close friends say they're not sure if they've seen them.

BOTH

SKB: **Let's hear one anecdote from each of you about something crazy, scary, or funny that happened during the making of one of your films.**

MB: As guerilla filmmakers, we're not afforded the luxury of "quiet on the set" that a studio provides. Shooting outdoors, especially, can be incredibly daunting—and was for us, on several occasions—when looping dialogue later isn't a feasible option. On *Runaway Terror*, for instance, the neighborhood seemed to erupt into an explosion of background noise every time I said "action": squirrels; wood chippers; cicadas; crickets; birds; dogs; cars; kids; basketball and/or baseball players.... At some point I decided to stop stressing about it, and a number of these sounds can still be heard in the final film(s). Naturally, critics would call this the makings of an amateur production. Whatever. In the end, I left them in because I felt they added realism to the scene.

RM: While making *Expendable*, we needed a few more exterior shots. On a whim, we pulled into the parking lot of a nearby church and began setting up the camera. Mark suddenly noticed two people eyeing us suspiciously from a far door of the church. It was about 9 p.m., so we didn't expect anyone to be there, much less notice us. We decided to grab at least one shot and go, but before we could break down our equipment, a police car pulled into the lot behind us. As the two people looked on from a distance, we had to show the cop our licenses and business card to prove who we were. It was a tense moment, and ironic that we should be questioned by the police for something so innocent!

Appendix Three

Words From the Players

Ryli Morgan

I was interested in the entertainment industry at a very young age, around five years old. I knew that I either wanted to model, act, or sing—if not all of the above. I would put on shows for the next-door neighbors, and of course, I'd remember to charge admission. Literally, it was just a childhood dream, and I finally got the opportunity to do it.

In 1999, I met Mark online. He sent me the equivalent of a three-page letter, telling me all about himself; his interests, what he does… He was doing music, at the time. We shared many interests, and eventually—after establishing a personal relationship—started making our own movies together. This was after he had tried his hand at screenwriting (he even had a manager in Los Angeles), but it just wasn't working out. I don't know if she was pitching them to the wrong people, or if there was simply no Hollywood interest in his work.

Either way, it only motivated us to proceed on our own, relying on no one but ourselves. We both shared the same dream and desire—from as far back as we could remember. Just because of that, I really think we were destined to be together. We mesh really well. Of course, it can be tough working together as husband and wife, since we're with each other all the time. It also helps to get the job done, though, because we're both so determined to do everything and get it done right.

JAMI HARRELSON (*RUNAWAY TERROR*; *THE ZOMBIE ROOM*)

From the time Mark and I started working together at what he calls his "day job," we hit it off from the get-go. What drew me into his world of filmmaking, more than anything, was seeing the passion he had for it... how much he cared about it. Seeing somebody with that kind of heart, and that determination to do something... it rubs off on you.

Runaway Terror was a learning experience for all of us, and Mark had to use whatever he had at his disposal, but it was obvious that he was getting the hang of things as we went along. We had a good time doing the film, even though things didn't work out like Mark wanted, at the end. He and Ryli had to finish it all on their own. I felt bad about it, but I had other obligations come up that couldn't be avoided. If I had to do things all over again, it would be different. All in all, though, I think everything with that one turned out as it was meant to be.

With *The Zombie Room*, Mark put what he'd learned on *Runaway Terror* to good use. At the same time, we were trying to rush through it. I think there was a lot of potential, there... except, in my makeup, I looked like the Tin Man!

We found an awesome location—that house was perfect—but we had to drive an hour and a half to get there. We tried, made the effort, but the distance and the stress involved got to everybody. Plus, I had the added stress of being in a rocky relationship. She and I were fine during *Runaway Terror*, but she wouldn't let me out of her sight, by then.

I remember we'd discuss things, like how Mark wanted to shoot something, and he'd allow me to offer my input. That's what made it feel like I was a part of something. He would listen, and we would change things... I've always tried to do the same, ever since.

We had some good laughs, too; joking around between takes. We had some good belly laughs. It was fun. Again, I just wish I wouldn't have been battling the stuff that I was. If I were to do it now, it'd be a different story. I'm a different person now. I was young and stupid, then, but as far as the experience altogether, I wouldn't trade it for anything.

Mark tells me he's said all he needed to with film, but I'd hate to see him get away from it completely. I've known him too long, though; something will inspire him eventually, and he'll come back to it. Anybody that creative needs an outlet, after awhile. I just hope he does it for himself, not for anybody else.

RACHELLE WILLIAMS (*EXPENDABLE*; *SIN BY MURDER*; *THE POWERFUL PLAY*; *HEAVEN HELP ME, I'M IN LOVE*; *HARDLY BELOVED*)

I never ask friends for help—and I should. God knows, I have many wonderful comrades who often tell me if I need anything, want anything—just ask. But it's some sort of pesky pride point and I just have to do the task, whatever it is, all by myself. Whether acting or writing, traveling or education… You know, I have to prove something… to someone… somewhere. As I get older, though, I am finally learning how to ask for help.

Acting was always a thing for me: I have fond memories of performing for my ridiculously patient grandmother in her kitchen, probably between the ages of six and seven, so she could judge my talents under various pseudonyms I scored from food products. (Really, my earliest nom de guerre, that I can recall, was "Sanka".) That early lucidity might explain why acting was always just something I did: for fun, for a creative outlet, for therapy, in a way. I never considered doing it *for real*, you know, for a day job. I was going to college, I was going to get a doctorate, then a "jobby job," write a bestseller in my downtime, find a cute and talented significant other, a nice loft, and you know, be admired or something for giving back to a planet which, at six or seven years of age, had not yet completely left me an angry, disillusioned, sneering female suffering the ravages of anomie. I did not need a five-year plan—I had a lifetime plan.

Note "marriage" and "babies" were not a part of the above life plan equation. I knew early on my American Dream was not the common ambition, and thus I tailored it accordingly.

So, much of the above itinerary has actually happened… or not happened, as the plan went, and I might actually still be working on that bestseller. But it's okay, because sometime during 2003, right around my twenty-fifth birthday, after I had graduated from the Honors College of Kent State University, and right before I slammed into my graduate program at Antioch University McGregor, something extraordinary happened: a phone call, a hunch, and a little detour became the start of my own private road trip for the next decade.

I still remember where I was standing when I got the call (in the lobby of my high school sweetheart ex's family business). I still remember who called me (my dear friend, the Executive Editor of *Tucson Lifestyle* magazine, Scott Barker). I remember the nervousness, the excitement, and the spunk I had all those years ago. I just *knew* it was time, the right moment, finally to leap in and take a huge risk or never bring up the subject of acting again. Like when you meet someone for the first time and you know he or she is "the one." Well, I had the same feeling about that phone call, too. Even at twenty-five years old, I knew I did not want to grow old regretting things I had *not* done.

Barker had just interviewed actress Ryli Morgan, for a now defunct incarnate of then-popular industry magazine, *Femme Fatales/Sirens of Cinema*. He was smitten. I could hear it in his voice as he eagerly filled me in on Morgan's prowess in her first major film role, *Despair,* directed by her husband, Mark Baranowski. It was dark, Barker had warned me, but well worth the watch—and the two were now looking to fill a role for their next film, *Expendable,* a lesbian vampire movie (before the market was flooded by vamps, so it was a big, damn deal).

It was now or never, and I knew it. I also knew the risks involved: no formal training, and film is forever. Today, as I did a decade ago, I shut down ALL of the annoying voices—all of the sounds, from well-meaning loved ones to jealous boyfriends, saying it was mistake in myriad ways: nudity is bad, lesbians are bad, vampires are bad, what if someone sees, whatifwhatifwhatifwhatif… until I just had a headache from it all. I felt cornered, outnumbered, playground pushed around, and in the end, I did what I always do as a stubborn, only child and now adult: I took some Excedrin and did exactly whatever in the hell it was I wanted to do.

I had already innocently infiltrated the B-movie subculture, much earlier—around the age of nine—writing to both Linnea Quigley and Brinke Stevens via their respective fan clubs (nostalgically, I can recall the addresses were obtained through my local library) and establishing an early idolatry and friendship with two amazing women who did not judge their youngest fan, but instead embraced and encouraged her. Then later, networking before "networking" was a buzzword, and with a definite lack of the aforementioned innocence, those early age-learned skills would prove useful as journalist Rhonda honed her craft, and professionally stalked her celebrity interview prey. In fact, only two celebrities would slip through my grasp in my two decades of writing: Robin Rochelle Stille and Wendy O. Williams, both committing suicide only a few months before I attempted to initiate contact.

So it would be in a North Carolina restaurant parking lot a few weeks later, with a new boyfriend (although now another ex) who drove all night to get me to the set of my first feature film, with Baranowski and his wife at my side (smiling in the sun), where I would giddily negotiate my "and" billing, and where I decided on the spot to use a pseudonym: I signed my first contract as Rachelle Williams. It sounded catchy, it paid homage, and by God, I wanted my two deceased idols to be proud of me.

Really, what other newcomer can say she was introduced to a screen goddess named Ryli Morgan, who looked her up and down, smiled sweetly, and in a sweet Southern drawl proclaimed, "Nice rump," before shooting the first scene? No one else. Just me—Rachelle Williams.

I still carry the small, red-and-black leopard print suitcase I bought in North Carolina as a present to myself for completing my first film—for really doing it and not just dreaming about it. It goes with me when I visit Brinke in Los Angeles, when I go as a fan to horror conventions, and when I hit film sets now as a veteran—never forgetting that it was a phone call from Barker, my own dogged sense of adventure, and Mark and Ryli who offered me that first shot, who made me feel at ease, and who gave me a once-in-a-lifetime, perfect first film experience. That's more than most people ever get in a lifetime, truthfully.

I could probably write my own book about Mark and our film sets together, another about Ryli, another about Brinke, and still another about all of the other fabulous co-stars and directors I have been so privileged to work with, and who have given me enough old-age rocker memories to make me smile well past my prime.

Even though making it big was never part of the plan (I've never had the patience for day-to-day celebrity operations, and I would have already been jailed for assaulting and torturing paparazzi), actually, I *have* made it. I've made it further than most budding starlets get to go, I've worked with and met so many of my heroes, and I even shot my first film at an age considered "old" by Hollywood standards. I only wanted a chance to look at the B-movie culture from the inside, as a player—that was the original plan—but in the end, I received way more than that. Way more than I ever could have even hoped for.

PAISLEY BLACKBURN (*SIN BY MURDER* [AS JYLLYAN DIXON])

Hello! My name is Paisley Blackburn. I worked with Mark Baranowski and his beautiful wife, Ryli Morgan, on a movie called *Sin by Murder*, back in 2004. (Back then, I went by a different stage name—Jyllyan Dixon.)

I found out about the role from a casting website that covered the Carolinas, as I was living in South Carolina at the time. If I remember correctly, Mark had quite a few issues casting the film because he was located right in the middle of the Bible Belt, and the movie originally called for something like twelve sex scenes. He told me he talked the producer into accepting a lot less, because of his location! That's the way Mark rolled. He was a practical businessman in addition to being a talented filmmaker.

I had to do three of those sex scenes, and honestly, I felt so comfortable with Mark that there were no problems or insecurities on my part. He was extremely professional, and the sets were closed to only the cast and crew needed for the scenes. One thing that I think is important to know is that Mark and Ryli were pretty much the entire crew! They did a feature film with only a handful of people. If you think about it, that is pretty impressive. Imagine what he could have accomplished if he'd had some more help!

Quite a few of my friends—males, of course—have watched the movie, and they all have said that they really liked it. I'm not saying it wasn't without flaws, but it was pretty good considering that Mark was not only the crew, but he also played a role in the movie.

I've stayed in contact with Mark over the last ten years, and he is always positive and down-to-earth. He is a very talented artist. If you haven't checked out the charcoal drawings he has done, you need to. It is like looking at a photograph. Mark is one of those multi-talented people who will go very far in everything he does because he puts 200% of his effort into his projects, whatever they are, and it definitely shows. I would work with him again in a heartbeat. He is genuine. He is talented. He is affable. More importantly… he is a friend for life!

Michael Hicks (*Sin by Murder*; *The Powerful Play*; *Heaven Help Me, I'm in Love*; *Ill Times*; *Hardly Beloved*)

As a child, I was babysat by television and movies. I've always loved both, but movies, especially, have always been a big part of my life. I tried to make it as an actor, in the late 1980's; I went out to California, and then came back home, broke, within two weeks. So acting stayed on the back burner for some time.

Then I saw an article in *The Charlotte Observer*, about how Mark and Ryli were filming their own movies; kind of on-the-fly, low budget, something they were passionate about. I figured I'd call him up and see if he could use an actor. I may have even said I'd pay *him* if I could be in one of his movies.

I really appreciate the chances he's given me. I loved every minute, and wouldn't take a dime for it. Really, from the bottom of my heart. I just appreciate everything he's let me be in so far, everything he's done, and I would love to work on more projects with him.

TRACY ELLIS (*THE POWERFUL PLAY*)

Since I was a little girl, I've wanted to be an actress, a model, a singer, a dancer, a musician, a choreographer... pretty much everything. I've danced since I was three, I've been in a few commercials, and I was a featured extra in a 2001 film, *Shallow Hal*. I've done some modeling assignments, and many photo shoots. That's how I found Mark; on the One Model Place website, I browsed through the filmmakers.

We started working together on *The Powerful Play*—and it was great! I loved it! I had a blast... I laughed, and laughed, and laughed. It was just a lot of fun. Mark was so easy to work with. Laid back, flexible, but professional. Very professional.

JAMES MCGRIFF (*THE POWERFUL PLAY; ILL TIMES*)

I met Mark at work. I love my cameos in his movies. I wear my *Ill Times* t-shirts about once every two weeks. Every time I go to a function, I put on the one with me on it, and people be like, "Man, that look like you!"

I be like, "That *is* me!"

They like, "Naw, it ain't!"

I be like, "It *is*, look!"

And they like, "*Damn!*"

And I'm like, "Yeah, I've been in, like, three movies."

They like, "You think you the shit."

I'm like, "Damn right. Shit, if you played in a movie and got a shirt, you'd be wearing it, too. Look what you got on your shirt; you got on Kermit the Frog. I got a picture of me... I'm supportin' my *own* clothing line!"

I enjoyed myself, sitting on the curb for *The Powerful Play*... Pour a little bit here, pour a little bit there... I'm saying, I was getting my feet wet, but... other than that though, it was for a good cause.

You know, I like all the videos. On *Ill Times*, there was more to it. I like who my character was, and I loved the cast. Everybody in there, because you know, I'm a people person, anyway. Blue, the two sisters (I can't remember their names), Dennis, of course—you know, that's my right hand man, right there—and Todd, he was there. He's real cool.

What's the one with Blue, in *Hardly Beloved*? Yella? One named Blue, the other named Yella… Now, *he* was a funny cat. Every time they tried to open the cooler, it was like EHHHH! I wasn't in that one, though. I came through, just to show support… for the fine work that Mark does.

On *Ill Times*, I even had my son in it. I showed a couple people that, because they don't believe it, so… when I have a function at the house, then I'll pop it in, let them see the cameo.

I was comfortable, doing what I had to do. I enjoyed playing the person that I played, even going from Mark's house to the scene at the park, with Blue and Todd. I enjoyed it, because we ended up staying at Mark's house. I got there at like, 11:00, and ended up staying at the mug until at least about 9:00. That whole day was a perfect day. The shoot, being around good people, the family atmosphere—all that.

I think *Ill Times* was one of Mark's best movies. That mug had action packed in it. I think when he's not in his movies, he's better, because he's a better director. He's more hands-on, instead of… like, when he's in there, then he has to pause it, go do that, do that, set things up, and all that, but when he's more hands-on, he can stay focused.

LYNN LOWRY (*HEAVEN HELP ME, I'M IN LOVE*)

Mark had seen my website, or one of my films (I can't remember which), and contacted me on the Internet. He told me he enjoyed my work, and that he made films, himself. Then I emailed him back, and asked that he keep me in mind for his next one. In his following email, he informed me that he already had one in the works, which turned out to be *Heaven Help Me, I'm in Love*.

I thought it would be a horror film. So, I read to page twenty of the script, and started thinking, "Wow, who's gonna get killed? And how?" It was funny and poignant, though, which I found strange. By page forty, I thought, they'd better kill somebody, quick!

Pretty soon, I realized it was not from the horror genre, which was a refreshing surprise. It was really funny. I enjoyed reading it., and I looked forward to doing it.

The shooting experience was very good. It was interesting; I'd never quite done a process like that before. I usually do an entire scene in one take, so it was simpler, in a way, because I could focus on one line at a time... and, of course, the lead actor was wonderful to work with! Mark is very talented. I enjoyed working with him a lot.

TOM MCCAFFERY (*HEAVEN HELP ME, I'M IN LOVE*)

I had the pleasure of working with Mark on the production of *Heaven Help Me, I'm In Love*, and it was a great experience. I remember a take that got us laughing hysterically, to the point that delayed production for a few minutes. I enjoyed the laid-back atmosphere. That's a good quality to have, when it comes to making a film.

We crossed paths after I spotted a post on the Internet casting boards, calling for a last-minute replacement. I contacted Mark by email, and then later by phone. He emailed me the script, and I traveled to Charlotte from Wilmington, where I resided at the time. We started filming within a couple of days.

I feel good about that decision, and my hats off to Mark. He didn't know about my experience, or what I looked like, until I got to Charlotte. Just from talking to me on the phone, he was confident that I was the one to help him finish the production. I was very thankful for that, and I'm proud of what we put together.

ENGLAND SIMPSON (*HEAVEN HELP ME, I'M IN LOVE; ILL TIMES*)

What Mark Baranowski doesn't know is that I stalked him and his Scream Queen wife, Ryli Morgan, for a few months before approaching them at a convention in North Carolina. I was a new actress; I didn't know the etiquette on how to speak with a director about possibly working together. So, I made it my mission to approach Mark and Ryli at the convention and beg them for an audition. I made a game plan: I would buy a movie or CD from their table and then force my newly taken, "Glamour Shots"-quality headshot on them.

I'll admit, I was a bit leery, being familiar with Mark and Ryli's films. I knew that I wasn't the type of actress that would be featured in an On Mark Production. I was so green to the game. Other than a featured part in a local play, I had never done any acting before. Nonetheless, I was determined to work with Mark and Ryli (they're movers and shakers—my type of people!).

After a little chatting... and a little flirting, Mark promised me a small featured part in his latest film, *Heaven Help Me, I'm in Love*. I was ecstatic, but I wasn't claiming film stardom until I knew that he'd actually use me in his feature. A few weeks later, I was donning fishnets, stiletto heels, and a leather whip on an actual OMP set. It was love at first slap! Playing the dominatrix, Candace, was the start of a beautiful relationship.

Ten years and a few projects later, Mark and Ryli are still some of my favorite people to work with. On Mark Productions is the epitome of grassroots filmmaking. It's that old familiar that I am always seeking out while on film sets. It is home.

DENNIS COTHRAN (*ILL TIMES*; *HARDLY BELOVED*)

Mark and I were co-workers, always clowning, and acting silly. The boss would get mad, yelling, "You're having too much damn fun!"

I said, "That's crazy! You want us fightin', up in here, and drunk?"

Anyway, as far as the movies go, I just wanted to try it one time... for the experience. *Ill Times* was funny. I liked the bloopers. Especially when Mark was like, "Whoo! Whoo!" Boy, everybody loved that. I looked at him, I said, "What the hell? Your ass ain't gonna die up in here, 'cause I ain't givin' you no mouth-to-mouth resuscitation. I gotta go home!"

We had fun. I was looking forward to the scary movie. I was gonna be a black serial killer, just killing people. I was gonna kill black *and* white, I wasn't gonna to be discriminating. I was just gonna kill everybody.

HAYLEY MORAN (*ILL TIMES* [AS HAYLEY LAKEMAN])

When I first met Mark Baranowski it was because he came to me for a tattoo: a realistic, black and gray movie monster. He was charming and smooth, and had an air of humble confidence. After hours together during the tattoo, I found him easy to talk to, and a very interesting man; a moviemaker, a spiritual soul, an artist. I was immediately interested in seeing—and even being a part of—some up and coming project.

When I first saw one of his films, I admit I was taken aback. It was raw, it was dark, and it was a bit dirty... a good glimpse into the mind of a man who created art for the sake of it, seeming to capture ideas without over-producing them.

When he asked me to be an actor in *Ill Times*, I instantly said yes. The filming process was fast and fun, and pretty free. Mark doesn't do a take over and over, so the pressure is on to get it right the first time, if possible. He also assures that the film keeps what I would call a kind of "garage band" quality that remains raw and in the moment.

I've had a great time getting to know him since our first shared art endeavor, and I look forward to watching his success grow on the personal—as well as professional—front. Mark Baranowski is a hi-fi soul with a knack for a kind of rugged, lo-fi filmmaking that is a killer combination for creative intrigue.

PARIS SIMPSON (*ILL TIMES*)

They say there's always a reason to cross paths with people. Sort of a fate… a natural dynamic of life. I feel blessed to have crossed into the path, and experience the many dimensions, of Creator Mark Baranowski.

I met Mark while he was in production of *Heaven Help Me, I'm In Love*, which my sister, England, had a role in. I was just a visitor, an observer, of art coming to life. I was so fascinated, listening to Pink Floyd and watching Mark work his magic, as he was in the process of editing and putting the pieces of his work together.

I later had the honor of working with him as an actor in *Ill Times*, which touched on a deeper level of life, and its characters' life experiences, one vignette at a time. I'm excited to see what the future holds for Mark. His imagination and talent is endless.

SOFIYA SMIRNOVA (*MISTER DISSOLUTE*)

I met Mark at a horror convention while in Pittsburgh, about eight years back, when I first got involved with the indie horror industry. I walked around to get acquainted with the other guests, and we struck up a long conversation. Weeks later, he showcased my photographs in one of his music CDs, *The Reason I Put This Together*.

What first impressed me about Mark was his drive to create whatever comes to mind. Magic happens with anything he puts his heart and desire into; creativity forms and brings it to life. He is a talented artist, with a passion for producing music and writing screenplays, which he then transforms into films.

In 2009, Mark sent me a proposal for a role in his next production, *Mister Dissolute*. I was happy to accept. Although it wasn't a lengthy visit, the experience in getting to know him, to pick his brain, and to exchange ideas, was fascinating. I admire his tenacity to take a project from start to finish, and his hard work to make his dreams a reality. In this world, anyone can live but not actually be alive. Mark, I can say, is alive and living, and producing. He has a goal and mindset to make things happen—big or small—and his accomplishments are a motivation to me.

Through the years, we've kept in touch. He is a wonderful father and husband, and his wife is a doll. It was a blessing to cross paths with an artist full of the energy and determination it takes to make happen anything he desires.

PHILLIP SMITH (*MISTER DISSOLUTE*)

I caught wind of Mark's *Mister Dissolute* project while on location in Nashville, Tennessee, for a film called *HVAC Zombies*. My co-star, England Simpson, informed me of it, claiming it was already in progress. That may have been, but just in networking with her, I was given the opportunity to meet Mark and snag a small role in the film, as a hit man.

Small world, really, considering England already knew Mark well, and had worked with him in the past. Not to mention, another talent from *HVAC Zombies*, Maria Kil, was also cast in *Mister Dissolute* (although I didn't work with her directly, in Mark's film).

I fondly recall watching Mark while he acted out one of his scenes in *Mister Dissolute*. Some of his dialogue, which he'd written himself, was so outrageous that he was laughing almost hysterically. This resulted in a lot of takes. He was just enjoying himself so much that he couldn't help it.

My first impression of Mark was, "Wow, this guy is very enthusiastic about what he does!" He's also easy-going, and great to work with. I know sometimes the word artist is an overly used term, but Mark really is a true artist in every since of the word—not only as a filmmaker, but also musically. Plus, his charcoal drawings are no less than fantastic (a word I don't use lightly!). He truly is visionary.

They say, "When you're doing what you love, you never have to work." Mark is a perfect example of someone who loves what they do. He's become a great friend since the day we worked together on *Mister Dissolute*… I think well of him and his family, and I'll always look forward to helping him with his future projects.

About the Authors

SCOTT KENYON BARKER is the Executive Editor for *Tucson Lifestyle* magazine, *Tucson Lifestyle Home & Garden*, and a frequent freelance contributor to several film publications. He began writing at an early age, and sold his first short story to a national magazine soon after high school. While attending The University of Arizona, where he studied theater, he continued writing and began selling magazine articles to regional, national, and international publications. He has won awards from the Arizona Authors Association and the Arizona Press Club, and has taught magazine writing for Pima Community College (where he is an adjunct faculty member) and Tucson Open University.

Photo: Barker Archive.

His screenwriting efforts began in the mid-1980s, and by October 2013 he had completed twelve screenplays, which include a TV pilot, several action thrillers, horror movies, and an indie-style drama. Several of his screenplays have been competition finalists, and he has been invited to pitch to major studios.

He was the co-writer and co-producer for *From A Place of Darkness*, with John Savage and Natalie Zea, now available on Blu-Ray. He was also the writer/director and producer for *Dead On Site*, released on April 5, 2011, by Acort International/Maxim Media, and is currently in post-production on the horror/martial arts feature film, *The Z*.

In 1994, he was contacted by Globe Pequot Press to write a travel book, *Arizona Off The Beaten Path*. He also has ghostwritten for an industrial psychologist, as well as contributed the text for a photo essay book about Tucson.

The summer of 2003 saw a return to his roots in literary fiction, as he served as co-editor and contributor with Rhonda Baughman for the short story collection, *Quietly... But With Force*.

MARK BARANOWSKI

is a multifaceted artist and the head of On Mark Productions. Beginning with drawing while still a child in his hometown of Buffalo, New York, his creative pursuits would later include song, book & screenplay writing, and then film-making.

While honing his talent as a charcoal pencil artist, he recorded a wide range of music under such names as The Marksman, Awful Goodness, and Marquis. In 2000, he self-published a novella, *Tartarus, Book 1: Lot's Phantasms*, and a collection of lyrical poetry, *Words Seeking Music*. His second screenplay, which he wrote as a potential vehicle for Jean-Claude Van Damme,

Photo: Baranowski Archive.

awarded him the services of a Hollywood manager, while his spec sequel to John Carpenter's *The Thing* caused quite a stir at Universal Studios. However, when nothing became of either, he vowed to neither waste any more time or to rely on the "studio system" to achieve his goals. To this day, he has no regrets for making this decision.

A masochist at heart, he now willingly resides in Charlotte, North Carolina—part of the Bible Belt—where his films remain privately enjoyed by the same people who criticize them publicly.

For more about Mark and his work, visit his website, *www.createtolive.com*.